Praise for
Lawyers' Poker

"*Lawyers' Poker* is clear, entertaining, *and educational*. It is a treasure trove of valuable lessons in competent trial advocacy, the art of negotiation and ethics—all told in a page-turning, storytelling fashion. As a bonus, the reader will also be introduced to the art of poker playing! Indeed, the parallels drawn are accurate. Both the neophyte and seasoned lawyer will love this book."

—Thomas A. Demetrio,
Corboy & Demetrio, Member of the Inner Circle of Advocates

"*Lawyers' Poker* is a fascinating read, as with great wit, skill, and clarity Lubet moves from the poker room to the courtroom with impressive knowledge of the operation of both venues. As a veteran cross-examiner, I found Lubet's thesis 'straight' and his book 'flush' with clever insight. Indeed, I 'bet' I could argue the case he makes to a 'full house.'"

—Benjamin Brafman,
criminal defense lawyer

"Every lawyer should play his cards right by reading Lubet's book. It's a safe bet the reader will come away with some great lessons in a courtroom and maybe even a tip or two at the card table."

—Robert A. Clifford,
former Chair, ABA Section of Litigation

STEVEN LUBET

LAWYERS' POKER

52 Lessons
That Lawyers
Can Learn
from Card
Players

OXFORD
UNIVERSITY PRESS

OXFORD
UNIVERSITY PRESS

Oxford University Press, Inc., publishes works that further
Oxford University's objective of excellence
in research, scholarship, and education.

Oxford   New York
Auckland   Cape Town   Dar es Salaam   Hong Kong   Karachi
Kuala Lumpur   Madrid   Melbourne   Mexico City   Nairobi
New Delhi   Shanghai   Taipei   Toronto

With offices in
Argentina   Austria   Brazil   Chile   Czech Republic   France   Greece
Guatemala   Hungary   Italy   Japan   Poland   Portugal   Singapore
South Korea   Switzerland   Thailand   Turkey   Ukraine   Vietnam

First published by Oxford University Press, Inc., 2006
198 Madison Avenue, New York, NY 10016

www.oup.com

First issued as an Oxford University Press paperback, 2008

Oxford is a registered trademark of Oxford University Press

Library of Congress Cataloging-in-Publication Data
Lubet, Steven.
Lawyers' poker : 52 lessons that lawyers can learn from card players / Steven Lubet.
    p. cm.
Includes bibliographical references.
ISBN 978-0-19-536901-4 (pbk.)
1. Practice of law—United States. 2. Trial practice—United States.
3. Poker. I. Title.
KF300.Z9L83 2006
347.73'504—dc22   2005027220

9 8 7 6 5 4 3 2 1

Printed in the United States of America

To Natan and Sarah ♥

Acknowledgments

This book could never have been written without the encouragement of Dedi Felman, my editor at Oxford University Press, and we also had great fun working on it together. I am grateful to Eric Liebeler and Justin Foster for their poker insights, and to Michele Bové, Stacey Hamilton, Thomas Hankinson, Brooke Lewis, Natasa Lukic, Ann Nelson, and Merryl Sloane for their editorial and production assistance. The members of the Unicorn Roundtable made a series of pointlessly erudite suggestions, most of which I successfully ignored. The Spray Trust Fund of the Northwestern University School of Law provided generous financial support, for which I am extremely grateful.

As always, Linda Lipton made everything possible and worthwhile. She has been my perfect bride for nearly 30 years and counting.

Contents

introduction   3

DIAMONDS ♦ *Maximizing Your Winnings*   11

lesson 1: *Saving Bets*   15

lesson 2: *Expected Value*   17

lesson 3: *Don't Gamble*   20

lesson 4: *Depend on the Rabbit's Foot If You Will,
but Remember: It Didn't Work for the Rabbit*   22

lesson 5: *Opening Hands*   28

lesson 6: *Drawing Hands*   33

lesson 7: *Chasing Is for Dogs*   36

lesson 8: *Yardley's Law (and Darrow's Exception)*   41

lesson 9: *Losing It*   49

lesson 10: *Desperate Times*   56

lesson 11: *Volatility*   59

lesson 12: *Sunk Costs*   63

lesson 13: *Stakes Matter*   67

CLUBS ♣ *Controlling the Opposition* 73

lesson 1: *Fundamentalism* 77

lesson 2: *Know Why You Are Betting* 80

lesson 3: *Slow Playing* 85

lesson 4: *Bluffing* 90

lesson 5: *Reverse Bluffing* 94

lesson 6: *Semi-Bluffing* 97

lesson 7: *Overplaying* 103

lesson 8: *Calling Bluffs* 107

lesson 9: *Loose Wiring* 111

lesson 10: *Folding Winners* 115

lesson 11: *Establishing Patterns* 118

lesson 12: *Implication and Storytelling* 121

lesson 13: *Patience* 127

SPADES ♠ *Digging for Information* 131

lesson 1: *Knowledge Is Power* 134

lesson 2: *Taking Their Measure* 137

lesson 3: *Tells* 141

lesson 4: *Get What You Need* 146

lesson 5: *True Lies* 151

lesson 6: *That's Acting* 155

lesson 7: *Calling Bias* 157

lesson 8: *Paying Attention* 161

lesson 9: *Reading Value* 165

lesson 10: *Total Recall* 169

lesson 11: *The Unexpected* 175

contents

lesson 12: *Local Rules* 178

lesson 13: *Showing Your Hand* 181

HEARTS ♥ *Ethics and Character* 187

lesson 1: *Lying* 190

lesson 2: *Cheating* 196

lesson 3: *Scamming* 202

lesson 4: *Banking the Proceeds* 209

lesson 5: *The Right Stuff* 212

lesson 6: *Moral Hazards* 215

lesson 7: *Self-Control* 218

lesson 8: *Beginner's Luck* 224

lesson 9: *You Gotta Have Heart* 229

lesson 10: *Cards Speak* 232

lesson 11: *Cross-Examination Does Not Mean Angry Examination* 235

lesson 12: *Beautiful Losers* 241

lesson 13: *Poker Ain't Life* 246

rank of hands 247

glossary 249

notes 255

bibliography 269

index 273

LAWYERS' POKER ♣

INTRODUCTION

A young lawyer moved from the Indian Territories (now Oklahoma) to Texas, in the early spring of 1888. Eager to get started, he rented a small office and put his shingle on the door, but he still had to be admitted to practice. There were few law schools in those days, and there was no formal bar exam. Instead, each aspiring lawyer, whether a youngster or a newcomer, had to appear for a personal interview before the Texas Supreme Court.

Our young man made his way to Austin, apprehensive but ready for what he expected to be a rigorous examination by the notoriously hard-nosed justices. Surprisingly, however, they asked him only four questions: Had he studied Blackstone? Did he read the Bible? Did he know his Shakespeare? And could he play poker?

The first three questions were easy to understand. Blackstone's *Commentaries* was the basic reference book for lawyers everywhere; and on the frontier it was often just about the only source available. The Bible and Shakespeare, of course, were essential to understanding human nature, a necessary quality for successful law practice (then as now). But the poker question made him nervous. Gambling was a vice, so he was worried that the justices were accusing him of immoral conduct.

Still, he had to answer honestly. The lawyer reluctantly admitted that he was a more-than-occasional seven-card stud player, fearful that this might disqualify him in the eyes of the Texas justices. To his relief, however, they admitted him to practice on the spot.

Once he was safely sworn in, the young lawyer got up the nerve to ask the court about the poker question. "Your Honors," he said, "I know why you inquired about Blackstone, Shakespeare, and the Bible, but what on earth does poker have to do with the practice of law?"

The chief justice looked down from the bench and sternly replied, "Young man, how else do you expect to make a living during your first three years as a lawyer?"

The chief had a good point. Lawyering could be an uncertain enterprise in the thinly settled West, with paying clients few and far between. Most attorneys could not survive without a sideline, whether it was ranching, journalism, or dishwashing. There was no way to know whether this particular young lawyer was any good at running cattle or cleaning plates, so the justices helpfully suggested that he turn to poker—figuring that anyone tough enough to practice law in Texas would also be pretty sharp at the card table.

That assumption was right on the money. As we will see throughout this book, there is a deep symmetry between litigation and poker, both of which involve competitive decision making with incomplete information. The theory and practice of poker will be immediately recognizable by every attorney who has ever made a strategic choice in the face of uncertainty.

Lawyers must make a constant series of decisions based upon a mix of available and unknown facts. The most obvious decision is whether to settle or to proceed to trial, but there are also many other, smaller decisions along the way—which depositions to take, which motions to file, which theories to pursue, which questions to ask—each one influenced to one degree or another by opposing counsel's behavior.

Poker games are much the same. Each player must continually decide whether to raise, call, or fold without seeing some or all of the other players' cards. There is a certain amount of public information in the form of exposed cards (except in draw poker) and, more important, in the betting behavior and physical demeanor of the other players. The key strategy in poker is almost always to deceive the other players by misrepresenting your own cards—often by showing strength when your cards are weak (thus bluffing them into folding their hands) or by showing weakness when your cards are strong (thus encouraging them to keep betting when they cannot win). Even honesty in poker is deceptive. A strong hand played strongly allows you to bluff more easily later in the game. The best card players, like the best lawyers, have a knack for getting their adversaries to react exactly as they want, and that talent tends to separate the winners from the losers.

In poker, every mistake costs money. A card player of even moderate skill usually knows instantly when he has misplayed a hand. What's more, he is immediately able to calculate the exact cost of the mistake. Because poker involves a relatively small number of variables—there are only 52 cards in the deck and only three possible moves in each round of betting—a player can assess every aspect of his game ruthlessly and with considerable accuracy. It is hard to keep kidding yourself in serious poker. You either win or lose.

Lawyers have considerably more trouble with self-assessment, however, and not only because of ego involvement and self-delusion. Every lawsuit has thousands of factors, and no case exactly duplicates any other. Most litigation comes to a fairly indeterminate end via settlement, while ultimate negotiating positions remain unrevealed. Often it is difficult to say whether, and to what extent, you have truly won or lost. Even in those cases that go to verdict, producing a clear winner, there is no easy way to identify which decisions worked and which failed.

In law practice, the many, many dependent variables defy isolation. Consequently, even the most well-recognized truisms cannot be completely validated or falsified. Never ask a question unless you know the answer. Sounds right, of course, but can it be proven? Save your strongest argument for rebuttal. Makes sense again, but aren't there exceptions? The opening statement is the most important part of the trial. This one has become a legend, but is it really true?

Unlike lawyers' assumptions, poker maxims are constantly being tested and refined, which makes poker wisdom a great strategic guide for litigators. Many poker principles are based on clear mathematical calculations, and others have been validated in practice. Poker is played by as many as 60 million Americans (many of them lawyers), and every player has a cash incentive to improve the quality of his play. Thus, capable card players know the precise odds of filling an inside straight (they're crappy, better use caution) or completing a flush when you get three suited

cards in seven-card stud (pretty good, often worth betting).
In other words, poker wisdom rests on real insight into the
workings of a game that exploits hidden assets and strategic
disclosure.

And, just like litigation, poker is all about winning.

There are many poker tactics that can be applied to comparable situations in law practice. In fact, we frequently borrow the language of poker to describe litigation.

Almost every case begins with negotiation, when you really have to "keep your cards close to your vest." Of course, you will make a reasonable offer "for openers," realizing that you might eventually have to "sweeten the pot." Your opponent, however, might try to "raise the stakes" by implying that she has an "ace in the hole." Still, you will probably be willing to "ante up," figuring that you can "buck the odds" if you "play your cards right." After all, a "four flusher" like your opponent might well be "drawing to an inside straight," in which case you will just have to "call her bluff."

If no one "folds," you will eventually end up in court. That's okay with you, as long as you can get a "square deal" (but heaven help you if the judge is taking something "under the table"). Anyhow, you'll have to "play the hand you're dealt," even if your star witness is a "joker." You can handle the cross-examination of the opposing party, though she might turn out to be a "wild card," just so long as your opponent doesn't have "something up her sleeve." It's too late to "pass the buck," so you'd better hope you have a "winning hand" (and that you aren't playing with a "stacked deck"). Even if you are tempted to "bet the farm," it's probably better to keep your "poker face" and "stand pat." Just make sure that everything is "above board" and that no one is "dealing from the bottom of the deck." But however much money there is "on the table," there is no reason to "tip your hand" until the "showdown."

Of all the many variations on poker—five-card draw, seven-card stud, high-low split, and countless others—it is probably Texas Hold'em that most closely resembles litigation, because it is based upon a combination of concealed information and publicly shared evidence. Hold'em is a popular and challenging game in which each player must make the best possible five-card hand by using any combination of his own two hole cards and another five communal cards that are dealt face up for use by everyone. The hole cards are dealt first, followed by an initial round of betting. Then the first three community cards—called "the flop"—are dealt face up, followed by another betting round. Next comes another community card ("the turn" or "fourth street"), more betting, then the final face-up card ("the river" or "fifth street"), and one last betting round. As in litigation, most of the information (represented by the flop, the turn, and the river) is shared, and it is also equally available for common use. The most important facts (the "hole" or "pocket" cards), however, remain privately held, to be revealed (or withheld) as each player determines best.

As novelist and poker player James McManus put it, Texas Hold'em is a game of optimal strategies with imperfect information, requiring educated guesses under conditions of extreme uncertainty. It is a "distilled competition" in which the "best strategy involves probability, psychology, luck and budgetary acumen, but is never transparent." No trial lawyer could have said it better, and most of the examples in this book will be based on Texas Hold'em.

As the subtitle explains, this is primarily a book about law and law practice, drawing upon the accumulated experience and insights of masterful card players to demonstrate ways that lawyers can refine their tactics and techniques. Perhaps someday another writer will show that the exchange can also run the other way ("how cross-examination can improve your poker skills"), but that seems both doubtful and unnecessary. Unlike litigation, poker provides its own laboratory conditions—including the possibility of computer simulation—so there would be little reason for card players to study lawyers' tactics. Attorneys, on the other hand, have always had to be intellectually omnivorous, borrowing freely from disciplines as diverse as literature and economics. So it should be no surprise that proven poker strategies can be extremely useful to courtroom advocates, with the following 52 lessons divided into four broad categories: "Diamonds" (maximizing your winnings), "Clubs" (controlling the opposition), "Spades" (digging for information), and "Hearts" (ethics and character).

L egendary football coach Vince Lombardi once said that "winning isn't everything, it's the only thing." Card players and lawyers might add another proviso: It's how much you win that really matters. In an athletic competition (or an election, for that matter), the winner is usually quite happy to come away with a squeaker. In poker and litigation, however, the magnitude of victory can make a tremendous difference.

Poker players know that you can maximize your winnings by careful "hand selection," meaning that you must avoid playing potential losers while backing your likely winners (often called "premium hands") to the hilt. Lawyers could often benefit from the same approach, abandoning weak or questionable positions in order to concentrate on stronger claims. Some attorneys never figure out that simple lesson, but no one ever understood it better than Clarence Darrow.

In 1924, Darrow found himself defending one of the most notorious cases in the history of Chicago. Two wealthy teenagers, Nathan Leopold and Richard Loeb, both brilliant but also troubled and immature, had set out to commit the "perfect crime." After luring a young acquaintance, 14-year-old Bobby Franks, into a rented car, they murdered him with a chisel. Then they drove the body to a remote marsh where they attempted to disfigure its features with hydrochloric acid before concealing it in a drainage culvert. Returning to Chicago, they sent a ransom note to Bobby's parents, demanding $10,000 in "old, unmarked bills" for the kidnapped boy, who they claimed was alive and unharmed. Mr. Jacob Franks was getting ready to pay the kidnappers when he received word from the police that Bobby's body had been found.

Leopold and Loeb's perfect crime soon unraveled completely, as investigators discovered Leopold's horn-rimmed glasses at the crime scene. Both boys eventually confessed under intense interrogation, each blaming the other for the actual killing.

Cook County state's attorney Robert Crowe filed capital murder charges against Leopold and Loeb, seeking their execution by hanging. Public sentiment was strongly in favor of the death penalty, no doubt fueled by the fact that the defendants came from such privileged and wealthy backgrounds.

Anticipating an insanity defense, Prosecutor Crowe began lining up psychiatric experts from across the country. Meticulously preparing his case, Crowe was confident that he could prove the defendants' guilt (he had both physical evidence and confessions) as well as their sanity. He also secured a substantial tactical advantage by indicting both defendants on multiple counts—murder and kidnapping—each of which carried the death penalty. Under the law at the time, he would have been able to bring the charges successively, thus giving him two opportunities to hang the defendants.

Darrow, however, was a master tactician himself. Recognizing the near futility of defending the case on the merits, he convinced both clients to plead guilty to the charges, thus allowing him to concentrate on saving their lives. The sentencing hearing lasted for a month, with more than 100 witnesses testifying about the facts of the crime and the defendants' mental states. Following the evidence, Darrow presented a 12-hour summation, thought by many to have been the finest argument ever given in an American court. He emphasized the defendants' youth and railed against the barbarism of the death penalty, calling upon the judge to be "kinder, more humane, and more considerate than the mad act of these two boys." At the end of Darrow's speech, Judge John Caverly was openly weeping, and the courtroom spectators sat in stunned silence.

Prosecutor Crowe responded with sarcasm and invective, attacking defense counsel (Darrow and a colleague) as "the distinguished gentlemen whose profession it is to protect murder in Cook County, and concerning whose health thieves inquire before they go out and commit a crime." The defendants, he said, were "cowardly perverts," "snakes," "atheists," and "mad dogs," while the defense psychiatrists were all prostitutes.

Two weeks later, Judge Caverly delivered his opinion. Although they had committed a "crime of singular atrocity," Leopold and Loeb would not die.

Technically, Robert Crowe won the case. Leopold and Loeb were both convicted of murder and sentenced to life plus 99 years in prison.[1] But of course, the greater prize eluded

[1] Loeb was murdered in prison in 1936. Leopold was paroled in 1958, after serving 33 years.

him. For the prosecution, true success could only have been achieved by obtaining the death penalty, and the lesser sentences were surely regarded as hardly a triumph at all.

In other words, Crowe was unable to maximize his victory, despite his strong hand. He probably alienated Judge Caverly with his strident sarcasm, and he definitely relied far too much on the gruesome facts of the case, failing to take the psychiatric testimony seriously.

Darrow, in contrast, realized that he could only win by minimizing his losses. By conceding the issue of guilt and declining to raise a pure defense of insanity, he was able to present his case in the most favorable possible light, while rendering much of the prosecution case irrelevant.

As every card player and lawyer should understand, you can only maximize your winnings by taking the long view. In contests where almost no outcome is ever certain, the key to success invariably lies in avoiding unnecessary losses, choosing your battles, and exploiting favorable opportunities. The first step, as Clarence Darrow showed us, is to stay out of losing situations. In poker, that is called "saving bets."

LESSON 1: *Saving Bets*

The first, and potentially most difficult, lesson for every poker player is that the bets you don't make are at least as important as the ones you do. Maybe more. Since you cannot possibly win every hand, or even a large plurality of hands, it is essential to minimize your losses when you are dealt weak cards.

It costs money to play a hand, and more money the longer you stay in it. Consequently, it saves money to fold a bad hand as early as possible, and it saves the most money if you fold before calling a single bet. A common strategy, therefore, is to play only premium hands, meaning those that you have the best chance of winning.

This approach is called "tight" play, and it is not without some problems, but it is far better than the frequently seen alternative of calling a few early bets and then folding when the action becomes more intense. Those first few futile bets are virtually wasted money, and they can add up significantly over the course of a game. It is usually far better to select a few potential winners and then play them through to the end, while sitting out all of the rest.

Many lawyers have the same sort of difficulty restricting themselves to premium hands, usually out of insecurity. Rather than draft a sturdy, single-count complaint, for example, a lawyer will freight it up with multiple counts, many of which simply repeat the same basic allegations, primarily for fear of waiving a valid claim. The same insecurity leads counsel to overload appellate briefs with numerous trivial arguments, rather than concentrate on a few good ones.

Of course, all of the handbooks caution against this sort of "loose play," warning that unnecessary claims and arguments inevitably detract from the good ones. Still, lawyers keep doing it, no doubt because the cost is invisible. No court would explicitly base its judgment on the inclusion of a trivial or futile argument in the losing party's brief. Though the wasted words, in an age of increasingly strict page limits, would have been better spent on more salient points, there is little way to reckon the direct price of flabby drafting.

As one poker maven observed, complex events (such as Texas Hold'em and, though he didn't say it, judicial decisions) are highly sensitive to initial conditions. His conclusion, equally applicable to poker and law, is that "the best

way to control chaos is at the beginning of the event." Folding a bad hand, or eliminating a pointless argument, will
invariably limit future losses. It is therefore an "invisible
form of winning."

Nonetheless, lawyers continue to ignore the sage advice
of their elders and the exasperated entreaties of the courts,
larding their briefs and pleadings with repetitive and feckless
verbiage. A few hours at the card table, however, might better
drive home the virtues of tighter play.

LESSON 2: *Expected Value*

If poker's first lesson is to reduce betting on bad hands, the
second lesson must be how to recognize good ones. There
are relatively few true premium hands, guaranteed winners
that should be exploited for all they are worth (a subtle art).
Then there are the playable hands, good enough for betting
in some situations but not in others, depending on the competition. How do you decide whether to bet—and how much
to bet—on a playable hand?

Poker players rely on the concepts of "pot odds" and
"expected value," which define the relationship between risk
and gain. In even the simplest situation, you need to consider three variables in order to determine the relevant odds:
the amount of the raise, the likelihood of success, and the
size of the pot. For example, imagine that you are holding
four cards to an open-ended straight, with one card yet to
be dealt. Your chance of completing the straight is 17.4%,
roughly five to one. Now assume that there has been a bet to
you of $10, and you must decide whether to call or fold. Are
you willing to risk $10 on a five-to-one shot? It depends on

the payoff—in this case, the size of the pot. Only if the pot is larger than $60 does the bet have a positive expected value, in which case you should call (or perhaps even raise). Otherwise, it has a negative expectation, and you should fold.

The expected value of a bet is not dependent on winning or losing the specific hand. In the example above, the odds are that such a hand will lose five out of six times, with a total cost of $50. Winning the sixth time, however, brings in $60, for a net gain of $10. The bet is worth making because it has a positive expectation—and the bigger the pot, the greater the expected value. The crucial calculation is whether the play will win sufficiently more when it works than it will lose when it fails.

The concepts of pot odds and expected value are also tremendously useful for lawyers. They can help us to see beyond some timeworn axioms, finding opportunity where it might otherwise have eluded us. For example, everyone recognizes the ancient admonition to cross-examiners: Don't ask a question unless you know the answer. This fits right in with the first rule of poker, which is to minimize your bets—playing only premium hands and asking only surefire questions. But just as the idea of expected value expands the universe of playable hands, it also increases the number of viable questions.

Imagine that you represent the plaintiff in an intersection accident case and that you have called the defendant driver to testify as an adverse witness. Assume also that—for whatever reason—the defendant's deposition was never taken, so you do not know the answers to many important questions. Applying the usual principles of cross-examination, you would not ask whether the defendant had his brakes checked in the previous 12 months, because you cannot control the answer.

Following poker theory, however, you would quickly see that the question might have a positive expectation. Perhaps nine out of ten times, the defendant will reply that his brakes were recently checked, meaning that your bet failed. Nonetheless, the loss is minimal, since the driver might still have been negligent in many other ways. In the tenth case, where the witness admits lax maintenance, the gain is substantial. It was a good question because of its positive expected value.

But not every unpredictable question is worth asking; some have negative expected value. Assume that you ask the driver a sketchier question: Was he speeding on the way to an illicit affair? His negative reply will no doubt be delivered with a good deal of appropriate indignation, and the judge might even rebuke you for your lack of a good-faith basis for the question. The damage to your credibility will be considerably greater than the expected gain from such a stab in the dark. True, the occasional positive answer would hurt the defense, but that would not be nearly enough to outweigh the damage from the many times you will come up empty.

A poker player would characterize the difference between these two questions—auto maintenance versus adultery—as a distinction between betting for value and betting for action. The first question is tightly controlled; the only possible answers are yes and no, either one of which can be accommodated. Its expected value is both positive and predictable. In contrast, the second question is highly volatile. It unleashes a host of exciting possibilities, but nearly all of them are unfavorable. It is audacious, but not valuable.

Maximizing Your Winnings

In his book *Poker Nation: A High-Stakes, Low-Life Adventure into the Heart of a Gambling Country*, Andy Bellin tells the story of Crazy Rich, a New York City poker player who did not understand the difference between betting and gambling. According to the dictionary, a bet is "[a]n agreement between two persons or sides that the one proved wrong about an outcome or fact will . . . pay a stipulated sum of money to the other." Gambling, on the other hand, means "play[ing] games of chance for money." The distinction is crucial: All gambling involves betting, but not every bet is a gamble. It all depends on how much control you have over the result and how much you are willing to trust your luck.

In poker, the best players do not depend at all on luck. Based on their ability to calculate precise odds, they bet only on positive expectations and predictable outcomes; either they hold unbeatable cards ("the nuts," in poker slang) or they are able to make other players believe that they do.[2] The worst players gamble, betting that they can get lucky and fill their hands.

Crazy Rich was a bad player of the worst sort (or maybe the best sort, if you were playing against him). Although he was brilliant in every other aspect of his life, a successful investment banker with a J.D. and an M.B.A. from an Ivy League school, he could never bring himself to fold a hand unless there was absolutely no possibility of winning.

---

[2] Hence, the famous line in the W. C. Fields film *My Little Chickadee*:
     TENDERFOOT: Is this a game of chance?
     FIELDS: Not the way I play it.

As in most casinos and New York card rooms, Crazy Rich's preferred game was Texas Hold'em, which he played recklessly. More often than not, he would stick around to see the last card, making bets and calling raises, even when it was obvious that he was holding a hopeless hand. When better players would have folded before the flop, Rich would keep playing. And when the flop didn't help him, he would still continue betting. After all, there was always the chance that he would draw the last two clubs to his three-flush or fill an elusive inside straight. Hence, Bellin made the observation that Rich would "bet his liver to see the river." It was not a compliment.

In poker, gamblers like Rich, even the most brilliant ones, always lose in the long run (and usually in the short run as well). As writer Anthony Holden explains, "Poker, I had always argued, was not a form of gambling; on the contrary, gambling was a *style* of playing poker—a loose and losing style at that."

The same holds true in litigation. A lawyer's job is to reduce risk for his client, not take chances on it. We see this principle in the often-repeated admonition that a cross-examiner must never ask a question if she doesn't know the answer. Asking a question out of curiosity is the equivalent of hoping to fill your hand on the river: You might get a good outcome, but don't bet on it. The chance of a damaging reply is at least 50-50, and often worse.

There is also a less well recognized corollary to the principle. As much as lawyers should avoid open questions on cross-examination, they should utilize them freely during depositions. Here, every inquiry pays off, since virtually any answer may turn out to be valuable. In fact, the lawyer has at least three ways to win. First, the answer to the open question may be helpful, providing information that supports the lawyer's case. Second, even a bad answer provides data that can be used in evaluating settlement strategy (and better to know it sooner rather than later). Finally, advance knowledge of even the most devastating fact can assist the lawyer in preparing for trial. In other words, depositions demand curiosity; there is almost no gambling involved.

And, of course, depending on what you learn in discovery, you just might decide to settle the case—folding your hand long before you see the river. Alas, Crazy Rich never learned that lesson. As his poker losses mounted, he began "borrowing" money from client accounts, figuring that his luck was bound to change. He ended up a fugitive, which is a pretty steep price to pay for gambling.

LESSON 4: *Depend on the Rabbit's Foot If You Will, but Remember: It Didn't Work for the Rabbit*

There are several more points that need to be made about the role of gambling (and luck) in litigation.

First, it is always possible to catch a lucky break. Sometimes, a document request will turn up absolutely nothing, and sometimes it will reveal a virtual gold mine. Sometimes, an adverse party will admit nothing in his deposition, and sometimes he will spill his guts. Sometimes, your star witness will be nervous and hesitant on the stand, and sometimes she will shine like a star. In a sense, every good result is lucky, given the ever-present threat of an unfortunate alternative. But, of course, there is more to it than that. Case-breaking documents are only disclosed when the discovery request has been thorough and exhaustive. Deponents are more likely to be forthcoming when the questions are probing and well designed. A witness can overcome her anxiety when she knows exactly what to expect on cross-examination. In these situations, and others like them, fortune favors the well prepared.

It could be said, therefore, that good lawyers (like good card players) are never truly lucky, because they always position themselves to exploit positive expectations. Yes, a professional player might take a chance on a five-to-one draw, but only when he has calculated the pot odds and knows that the payoff would be six to one or better. He is not lucky when he hits his card, any more than he is unlucky when he draws a worthless card and throws away his hand. Rather, he has played the odds correctly, win or lose, and has assured himself a profit in the long run. Likewise, a capable lawyer is not really lucky when a surprisingly cooperative witness agrees with every proposition on cross-examination. Instead, she has benefited, as the saying goes, from the intersection of preparation and opportunity. A forthcoming witness is a wonder to behold (and to lead and exploit), but you will not know which questions to ask unless you have done your homework.

By the same token, bad lawyers are seldom unlucky. Their misfortunes are generally their own doing, born of poor planning and unrealistic expectations. Even an occasional stroke of good luck will frequently turn out badly for an incompetent lawyer, because it will only encourage him to continue making poor choices. In poker, it is often said that lucky breaks keep suckers at the table. They would not continue playing bad cards unless they occasionally hit big. A weak player who draws out on the river is likely to lose it all chasing the next few hands.

Maximizing Your Winnings

It is easy to imagine a lawyer in a similar situation. We all know it is a mistake to ask a witness to explain an inconsistency on cross-examination, rather than to let the contradiction speak for itself (and to make good use of it in final argument). Some lawyers, however, cannot resist the temptation. Usually they regret it when the witness delivers a well-deserved zinger. Every now and then, however, the question will pay off, provoking an outlandish or incoherent explanation that undermines the witness's credibility. But bad lawyers being, well, bad lawyers, they ultimately learn the wrong lesson. Rather than thanking their stars and swearing off the dangerous habit, they conclude that they are somehow blessed with the ability to know when to break the rules. "Explanation questions just work for me," they say, oblivious to the lurking, and certain, disasters.

Before we dismiss luck entirely, there is one way that it might be said to play a crucial role in both poker and law—the confluence of second-best hands. As we have seen, it is *not* really lucky to draw pocket aces in Texas Hold'em; it is just your turn, as everyone else will eventually get the same cards the same number of times. Your result, with aces or any lesser hand, primarily depends on how well you play your cards. But it *is* lucky (or luckier) if someone else at the table draws pocket kings at the same time, because that will build up the pot. Conversely, it is relatively unlucky if everyone else at the table draws unplayable rags, because your aces will not be worth much if all of the other players fold their hands. The stronger the second-best hand, the luckier you are.

Litigation works nearly the same way. Good lawyers make the best of their opportunities, regardless of fortune or chance, but it *is* lucky when the opposing attorneys overplay their own hands or make thoughtless mistakes. An excel-

lent example occurred in the 1949 perjury trial of Alger Hiss.
Many historians believe that the Hiss trial set the stage for
the McCarthy era that followed, but the prosecution might
well have failed if the defense had not staked its case on a
second-best hand.

Alger Hiss had been a high official in the U.S. Department of State during and after World War II. He had played
an important role at the Dumbarton Oaks Conference,
which initiated the organization of the United Nations, and
he also served on the U.S. delegation to the Yalta Conference,
the wartime meeting that drew the postwar map of Eastern
Europe. By 1948, Hiss had left the government and was serving as president of the Carnegie Endowment. He was at the
pinnacle of his career, a virtual avatar of the American political establishment.

In August 1948, however, a former Communist party
functionary named Whittaker Chambers denounced Hiss
to the House Un-American Activities Committee (HUAC),
claiming that Hiss had actually been a member of an underground Communist cell that had infiltrated the government. Hiss insisted on appearing before HUAC, where he
adamantly denied the accusation. He soon sued Chambers
for defamation, but his case fell apart when Chambers produced handwritten and typed documents (the so-called
Pumpkin Papers), evidently transmitted by Hiss, that backed
up Chambers's claims. Hiss was indicted for perjury, based
on his earlier sworn denial that he had ever given any documents to Chambers.

The prosecution case was based on Chambers's testimony
and, of course, on the Pumpkin Papers. The defense countered by challenging Chambers's credibility, charging that he
had faked the documents and lied on the stand. Compared

to Hiss, Chambers was certainly a questionable witness; he was, after all, an admitted Communist with a spotty past. In contrast, the patrician Hiss had enjoyed an impressive career at the very heights of society in Washington, D.C. Character witnesses on his behalf included two justices of the U.S. Supreme Court (Felix Frankfurter and Stanley Reed), a past candidate for president of the United States (John W. Davis), and the governor of Illinois (Adlai Stevenson II, who would later run twice for president).

But while Hiss's character witnesses were unimpeachable, that was not the case for his psychiatric expert, Dr. Carl A. Binger, who testified that Chambers was a "psychopathic personality" and a "pathological liar." Binger, however, had never examined Chambers, but instead based his diagnosis on a review of Chambers's personal history and his demeanor on the witness stand.

The cross-examination fell to Assistant U.S. Attorney Thomas Murphy, and it was a daunting task. Dr. Binger was well educated, articulate, and self-assured. He was not going to be a pushover. Murphy realized that he could never shake Binger's overall opinion, questionable as it was, so he opted for a different tactic. Instead of launching a frontal assault, he would instead isolate the individual bases for Binger's opinion, attempting to show that each one provided inadequate support for the "psychopathic personality" diagnosis. That approach required exquisite control of the witness, making sure that he answered the questions only on the narrowest possible terms. Given the slightest latitude, Binger would surely have expounded about Chambers's supposed propensity toward fabrication, but Murphy's carefully crafted questions kept the witness under tight control.

For example, Binger had testified on direct examination about Chambers's history of bizarre and erratic behavior. It was significant, Binger said, that Chambers had dropped out of Williams College on only the second day of his freshman year, abandoning the dormitory at midnight. Binger's point, of course, was that a less impulsive (and therefore more "normal") person would at least have waited until morning. But Murphy would not give the witness an opportunity to explain. Instead, he closely cabined his questions, concentrating on the railroad schedule, rather than on Chambers's inexplicable and hasty departure from school.

QUESTION: I think you said that leaving Williams College impulsively was bizarre. . . . Well, is it bizarre, Doctor, under your definition?

ANSWER: Relatively.

Q: When you testified that he left—I think you said he left impulsively. Did you assume that as one of the facts, that he left impulsively?

A: Yes.

Q: And you said that what was bizarre was the fact that he left at midnight to catch a midnight train. Do all people who catch midnight trains, Doctor, exhibit bizarre behavior at all?

A: They could. They don't need to necessarily. It depends upon why they do it.

Q: Doctor, you have been in the Grand Central [Station] at midnight, haven't you?

A: Yes.

Q: All those people running and scurrying for trains, you would not ascribe to them bizarre behavior?

A: I wouldn't have any idea what the meaning of their behavior was.

Q: Doctor, the testimony is that he got a midnight train; [there is] nothing bizarre about that by itself, is there?

Binger had no alternative but to agree, and thus one of the props of his opinion was neatly knocked away. Murphy used this same technique throughout his cross-examination, all but shredding the witness's confidence along with his diagnosis.

In a one-on-one "swearing contest" between Hiss and Chambers, there was a decent chance that Hiss would win. He was suave where Chambers was rough-edged; he was accomplished and respected while Chambers's life had been a wreck. But the defendant's hopes of acquittal sank along with Dr. Binger's credibility. One commentator observed, "Mr. Murphy just wanted plain answers to plain questions— about the most alarming assignment anyone would wish on a psychiatrist."

Hiss's counsel had blundered badly by putting the psychiatrist on the stand. Binger's testimony turned out to be decidedly second-rate, and he dragged the rest of the defense down with him. Murphy was an outstanding cross-examiner, well prepared and incisive, but he was also very lucky that the defense strategy provided him with such an inviting target.

LESSON 5: *Opening Hands*

Poker is a game of probabilities, and the probabilities are exactly the same for everyone. There is no such thing as a lucky player who consistently draws higher cards than everyone else, and there is no way (without cheating) to improve the odds in the long run. Good players don't win because they have better cards; they win because they play their cards better.

Good players also understand that the best cards at the beginning of a hand are usually going to be the best at the end. This is a matter of simple math. The odds of improving on a pocket pair (the first two cards, dealt face down) are the same, whether your cards are high or low. So the chance of drawing, say, a third six is exactly the same as drawing a third nine or a third queen (about 4% with one card to come, around 8% with two). The queens are obviously better to begin with, and the great likelihood is that they will stay better, even if someone at the table feels lucky. It is generally a losing proposition to stick around and bet against superior cards, unless you are an accomplished bluffer (more on that later).

In other words, cards are not intrinsically good or bad; they are only better or worse in relation to one another. A pair of kings might seem like a winner, but only if no one else has a pair of aces. A straight is usually a premium hand, unless there is a flush on the board. This is true of "drawing hands," as well, where your cards have great potential but no immediate value. Four suited cards, after the flop, will produce a flush 35% of the time, but they will lose to a low straight the other 65% of the time. And conversely, sometimes a pot can be stolen with a rag hand, when no one else has anything worth betting on.

It can be really risky, therefore, to fall in love with your cards just because they look good, or because they would have won an earlier hand. Unpaired jacks and queens can be especially dangerous. A couple of picture cards may seem promising, but there are too many ways that they can be beaten—by aces or kings or by any small pair. Even if you flop another jack or queen (or both), you will lose to someone who picks up the third card to any pocket pair. Therefore, you always have to ask yourself, especially when confronted by an aggressive pre-flop raise, "Do I have the best hand now?" Or, as the poker writer Ken Warren puts it, "if this were a two-card contest, who would win?" Pot odds, bluffing, or other sophisticated strategies can make it worthwhile to bet against a better hand, but those plays should be based on expected value.

This gives us several important insights regarding cross-examination. First, dragging out the questioning is not likely to make it better. If your examination begins badly, it will generally end badly, because a strong witness—with a powerful story and few apparent weaknesses—can rarely be rattled by an extended cross. You may not believe the witness, you may be frustrated by her unjustified show of confidence, you might have reasonably expected your initial questions to blow her out of the water, but there is seldom much to be gained by continuing to badger a tough witness.

There will be temptation, of course, to stick with a promising line of questioning, challenging the witness with preambles like "Do you really believe . . ." and "Yet you still say . . ." But those tactics are usually ineffectual, very much like betting against a stronger hand. Yes, you might sometimes succeed in shaking the witness or getting her to back off, but it is just as likely (and probably more so) that she will improve her own hand by deflecting the repeated jabs.

Ken Warren's query can be modified to work as well for lawyers as it does for card players: "If this were a two-question cross-examination, would it succeed?" If not, it is probably just as well to finish it up (though, again, there are some sophisticated strategies that might sometimes be worth pursuing).

That brings us to the second point. Poker players lose money by falling in love with their cards, and lawyers screw up by falling in love with their game plans. Strong witnesses tend to stay strong, so it is a mistake to stick with a prepared cross-examination just because it "should have" succeeded. No trial plan is intrinsically good; instead, it either works with a particular witness or it doesn't.

For example, it is often effective to impeach a witness, and a prior inconsistent statement can be as enticing to a trial lawyer as pocket jacks are to a card player. Imagine that a crime victim told the investigating police officer that he was mugged by a tall teenager with long hair. The defendant, however, turns out to be in his mid-20s, 5'9" tall, and short-haired. In preparing for trial, defense counsel would no doubt plan to confront the victim with his statement to the police, banking on undermining the identification and challenging the witness's credibility. That would be classic cross-examination, of a sort that has won many cases in the past.

But what if the witness's direct examination is truly compelling, describing the defendant in great detail, including the sound of his voice and the clothes that he was wearing when arrested? Suppose that the prosecutor got the witness to explain the seeming disparities about the defendant's age (he looked young), height ("I was knocked to the ground, so he must have seemed taller"), and hair length (maybe he cut it)? Now any attempted impeachment could just give the witness another opportunity to explain his testimony, strengthening the identification rather than weakening it. Whatever points might be scored about the defendant's age and hair might easily be overwhelmed by the witness's repeated testimony about being knocked off his feet and looking up at the grinning (and unforgettable) assailant.

It would still be tempting for the cross-examiner to go ahead with the planned impeachment, but it would probably be a mistake. Like pocket jacks, impeachment with a police report is usually a winner, worth betting on. But not always. In either case, you have to be ready to back off when there are stronger cards on the table.

And now a final point. While it is true that the best opening cards usually win a particular hand, no one ever consistently holds the best openers throughout an entire game. There will always be more hands in which every player has an equal chance of drawing pocket aces. Luck is going to even out, and better players will win in the long run.

While the lesson about strong openers gives us some guidance regarding individual witness examinations, it most certainly does not apply to an entire case. In fact, cases do get better in the course of litigation—through investigation, discovery, depositions, motion practice, negotiation, witness preparation, and just plain hard work. Weak cases have been known to improve dramatically, and strong cases often fall apart under pressure. A case in litigation is not like a single poker hand, but rather like an extended game—with multiple opportunities to make the right moves and lay the groundwork for future successes by surprising or outwitting your adversaries.

Good card players, and good lawyers, recognize that only long-term results matter in the end. That is why they do not try to win every hand.

The best openers usually win, but they do not always win. With five cards yet to come, there is always a good possibility that someone will draw a better hand.

The legendary Doyle "Texas Dolly" Brunson, two-time winner of the World Series of Poker and author of the justly celebrated *Super System* books, estimates that pocket aces will only end up winning about 50% of the time in a multi-player game. That clearly gives the aces a tremendous pro-spective value. But it also means that someone else will win the pot around half the time, usually because she success-fully played a drawing hand, completing a straight or a flush after the three-card flop. In fact, the best hands—straights, flushes, full houses—can only turn up on the flop (or later), so it makes sense to expect considerable betting on drawing hands, sometimes all the way to the river.

But which drawing hands are playable and which ones should be folded? The answer is always relative, depending on the strength of the competition, the size of the bet, and the pot odds. The first decision comes before the flop. Let's say you are holding a couple of medium connector cards, such as 9♣ and 10♥. That hand is a potential straight, though it will bust far more often than it will come through. A couple of big pre-flop raises therefore ought to make you extremely wary. It will be expensive to play the hand, and chances are good that you will be betting against a high pair or a better drawing hand (or both). If there is minimal pre-flop action, however, it might make sense to stick around for the flop, since you could see three additional cards for the price of a small bet. In reality, you have to decide how much you are willing to pay to see the next three cards, realizing that most of the time you will end up folding your hand in any event.

The calculation improves significantly if your connectors are also suited, such as 9♥ and 10♥. Now your chances of winning have more than doubled, since you can flop either a straight or a flush. The odds therefore improve proportionately, with the increase in the expected value of your hand. An aggressive player might bet strongly in this situation, driving out weaker drawing hands and improving his own chances to win. And he would bet even more aggressively if the suited connectors were higher, say Q♥ and K♥, since he would then be looking at an even better straight or flush, as well as the possibility of drawing a high pair.

If the price is cheap enough, or the odds good enough, it makes sense for a drawing hand to pay to see the flop. But don't get too optimistic. The chances of filling a hand on the flop are minuscule. The likelihood of completing a flush on the next three consecutive cards, for example, is less than 1%, and the chance of completing a straight (by drawing three more connectors) is only a little better. On the other hand, the odds are fairly decent that your drawing hand will improve, though remaining incomplete. A two-flush will flop into a four-flush around 10% of the time, and pocket connectors will turn into a four-straight about 25% of the time. And suited connectors will improve, one way or the other, more often than that. (You could also pair one or both of your pocket cards, but, then again, so could everyone else.) So almost any way you look at it, a pre-flop drawing hand is, at best, going to be a post-flop drawing hand as well, requiring some additional decision making and revised pot-odds calculations.

In a sense, every case is like a drawing hand because every case needs improvement. There are almost no sure winners in the world of litigation, but only cases with more or less potential, depending on how the cards fall. An effective lawyer is always looking for another witness or an additional document or a key admission that can increase the value of his hand, and he also must be ready to back away from a promising claim or a theory that doesn't quite pan out, even though it was worth pursuing for a while.

More to the point, an astute attorney will always be looking for ways to keep drawing cards at little or no cost. Just as a poker player wants to pay the minimum price to see the flop, a lawyer needs to balance the chances of improving his case against the cost of gathering further information.

Consider the deposition of an expert witness. If you have done your homework, you will be thoroughly familiar with the witness's professional background. You will have read all of her publications, and you may well have transcripts of testimony from her other cases. This material may not be devastating (most experts do not flatly contradict themselves), but it might well expose analytical weaknesses or potential inconsistencies. Or perhaps you managed to unearth something mildly embarrassing in the expert's past, such as a dismissal from a job or a scolding from a judge. Whatever the raw material, you will usually want to see how the witness reacts to it. She may be stunned and unnerved when confronted by her past words or deeds, or she may have a completely calm and reasonable explanation for the seeming inconsistency or faux pas.

In either case, that knowledge will be valuable as you gear up for trial, since it will allow you to take the witness's measure and prepare your cross-examination. But it will come at a cost. You will lose the advantage of surprise, and the witness will have plenty of time to recalibrate her reaction and revise her reply. An expert who sputtered incoherently at the deposition might turn into the very model of composure when answering the same questions in court. Then again, she might blurt out a damning admission in the deposition—"My God! How did you find that?"—which will be irreparable no matter how much time she has to reconsider.

As with all drawing hands, the chances of a big score are pretty small. Most witnesses will take things in stride, happily explaining the harmonious relationship between the paper trail and their current testimony. But now and then you will be rewarded by the sight of shaking hands and palpitations, or at least some overt discomfort, indicating that you have stumbled across some true vulnerabilities.

As is often the case in law and poker, the risk and reward are closely related, especially when you are making a speculative draw. The more stuff you have on the witness, the greater the likelihood of a payoff at the deposition—and the more you stand to lose by alerting her before trial. You can think of your background research as the equivalent of your pocket cards, and the witness's response as the equivalent of the flop. How much are you willing to risk by asking the next question? How badly do you want to see what happens?

LESSON 7: *Chasing Is for Dogs*

While poker has been widely played in the United States since the early nineteenth century, the game's modern era can probably be dated to 1949, when Nick "the Greek" Dandalos showed up in Las Vegas looking for a high-stakes, no-limit game. Claiming to have broken all of the high rollers in the East (including Arnold Rothstein, the man who fixed the 1919 World Series), the Greek wanted serious action—"the biggest game this world can offer"—so he sought out Benny Binion, owner of the Horseshoe Casino.

Binion himself had arrived in Las Vegas just three years earlier, abandoning his native Texas under considerable pressure from the local police. Having eked out a living as a bootlegger and gambler (and having beaten the rap on two different homicide charges), Binion took advantage of Nevada's gambling-friendly climate by purchasing the somewhat ragged Eldorado Casino, which he promptly renamed Binion's Horseshoe. Rather than trying to sell glitz and glamour to the tourist trade, Binion decided to appeal to serious gamblers by offering straightforward games and, as he proclaimed on a sign above the door, "The World's Highest Limits." Until recently, Binion's Horseshoe remained the world epicenter of serious poker, but that's getting slightly ahead of the story.

At the time, poker was not a big deal in Las Vegas. Played for relatively low stakes and strict limits, poker did not offer much profit to casinos since the players bet against each other rather than the house. Binion, however, saw the Greek's request as a great publicity opportunity, and he agreed to arrange the game, but only if it could be played near the casino entrance, rather than in the usual back room. And Benny Binion knew just the right opponent for Nick the Greek.

Johnny Moss was a professional poker player in his early 40s who had exhausted most of the competition in Texas. An old friend of Binion's, he jumped at the chance to play one on one in the biggest legal poker game in history. Driving all night from Dallas, Moss immediately sat down at the table with Dandalos, and the two men faced each other for the better part of five months, while crowds of rail birds stood around the table, amazed at the huge amounts of money changing hands. On the strength of that game, Moss and Dandalos became the world's first two poker celebrities, and Binion figured out that high-visibility poker was good for the gambling business in general. One hand in particular has become the stuff of legend.

The two men were playing five-card stud (one down and four up, with four rounds of betting), a game that was once quite popular but has since been nearly abandoned. Moss was dealt a nine in the hole with a six showing. Dandalos's up card was a seven. The first round of betting was reserved by no-limit standards, with Moss calling the Greek's $2,000 bet. On the next card, Moss drew a nine, giving him a pair. Dandalos caught a six, with no apparent improvement. Moss bet $5,000 on his nines, which beat any pair that Dandalos might have, but the Greek immediately raised $20,000, which Johnny called. "I'm figurin' to take all that money of his," Moss later remembered, "and I don't want to scare him none." On the next card, Dandalos drew a three and Moss drew a deuce, meaning that the nines were still good (although Dandalos was showing a possible straight). Moss made a huge bet, which Dandalos surprisingly called, putting more than $100,000 in the pot. Moss's final card was a three and Dandalos's a jack, busting his chance of a straight. Here is how Moss described the action:

> He's high now with the jack and he bets $50,000. I can't put him on no jack in the hole, you know. He ain't gonna bet all that money just for the chance to

outdraw me. I don't care what he catches, he's gotta beat those two nines of mine. So I move in with the rest of my money.

Moss shoved nearly $200,000 into the pot, assuming that the Greek would fold. Instead, Dandalos looked across the table and said, "Mr. Moss, I think I have a jack in the hole."

"Greek," answered Moss, "if you've got a jack down there, you're liable to win yourself one helluva pot."

Without speaking, Dandalos moved his own $200,000 to the center of the table and turned over his hole card: the jack of diamonds. He won over a half million dollars on a single hand.

"He outdrew me," Moss explained. "We had about $250,000 apiece in that pot, and he won it. But that's all right. That's better than all right. If he's gonna go chasin' dreams like that, I know I'm gonna break him in the end."

Indeed, that is what happened. After months more of around-the-clock play—breaking for sleep only once or twice a week—Johnny Moss built up a steady lead, winning pot after pot in the two-man game. Finally, the Greek decided that he'd lost enough. "Mr. Moss," he whispered, "I have to let you go." No records were kept, but it is said that Nick Dandalos lost nearly $2 million in five months of poker, an astonishing result, especially given that he had been ahead nearly $500,000 after drawing a second jack to beat Johnny's pair of nines.

But of course, that is the point of the story. Johnny Moss played his cards correctly from the start, knowing that his pair of nines beat anything in the Greek's hand. He bet aggressively right to the end, planning to make it too expensive for the Greek to stick around with his drawing hand. In fact, the Greek's cards were even worse than they appeared, since he never had a straight draw at all. Instead, the Greek was chasing a jack—one of only three cards, of the remaining 43 in the deck, that could help him. Until the last card was dealt, the Greek's chance of winning was less than 7%, while the pot odds were roughly even.

It was a risky play, even though it worked. Once. An approach like that will not succeed in the long run, which Johnny Moss immediately recognized. He wasn't happy about dropping $250,000, but he figured the Greek for a chaser—playing hunches instead of the cards—and he used that insight to drain the Greek's bankroll.

In 1970, when Benny Binion launched the World Series of Poker, he patterned the event on the Moss-Dandalos show-down. Fittingly, Johnny Moss won the first two champion-ships, and he won again in 1974.

Over the decades, the World Series of Poker expanded exponentially, from a relative handful of players in 1971 to more than 5,000 entrants in 2005. Benny Binion died in 1989, however, and his three children were not able to keep the casino running successfully, as is chronicled in James McManus's masterful book *Positively Fifth Street*. Eventually, Harrah's bought the rights to the World Series of Poker, though continuing to hold the event, at least in part, at Binion's Horseshoe (no longer owned by the Binion fam-ily). The 2005 WSOP, however, was the last one ever held at the original site; the entire competition is now part of the Harrah's empire.

For all of his luck, stamina, and nerve, Nick the Greek remains a footnote in poker history, remembered for win-ning a battle and losing the war. It is easy to be seduced by the occasional payoff of a bold and risky move. And once successful, it will be tempting to try it again (and again), heedless of the inevitable long-term losses. Card players and lawyers would both do well to reflect on the perils of chasing, rather than the allure. As Andy Bellin explains, "husbands get caught, dogs get run over, and card players go broke." The fabled Thomas "Amarillo Slim" Preston puts it more graphically, "I don't bet on hunches because I don't believe in hunches. Hunches are for dogs making love."

LESSON 8: *Yardley's Law (and Darrow's Exception)*

If Johnny Moss was the apostle of tight play, Herbert O. Yardley (1889–1958) was the prophet.

Yardley was a brilliant mathematician and spy, as well as a lifelong poker player. His first day job was as a code clerk with the U.S. State Department, where he quickly discovered his talent for numbers and cryptography. During World War I, he transferred to the cryptanalysis section of U.S. military intelligence (MI), serving with the American Expeditionary Forces in Europe. Following the war, Yardley continued to work for the army and the State Department, organizing the first peacetime cryptography service in the United States. Known only as MI-8, Yardley's clandestine group worked at deciphering foreign governments' diplomatic codes.

They had their greatest success when they broke the Japanese cipher and used that knowledge to intercept instructions from Tokyo to the Japanese delegates at the Washington Naval Conference in 1921–1922. Yardley passed the decrypts to Secretary of State Charles Evans Hughes—a former Supreme Court justice and future chief justice—who used them to outfox the Japanese negotiators, creating a

42
♦

naval advantage for the United States that would last until Pearl Harbor.

Despite this triumph and others like it, the State Department shut down MI-8 in 1929, when Secretary of State Henry Stimson famously remarked, "Gentlemen do not read each other's mail." Unemployed and disaffected, Yardley turned his hand to writing. In his memoir, *The American Black Chamber*, he revealed the existence of MI-8's secret cryptography program, including its continuing access to Japanese diplomatic dispatches. The book became an international bestseller, but it outraged U.S. Army intelligence (which had continued its code-breaking efforts), especially when the Japanese changed their cipher system. There was briefly talk of prosecution, but it turned out that the Espionage Act, as then written, did not cover cryptanalysis data (it was amended two years later). Yardley's second book, *Japanese Diplomatic Secrets*, was banned by an act of Congress, the first and only time that Congress voted to censor a specific book.

Yardley later worked as a cryptologist and cipher specialist for several foreign countries—most notably in China during the early years of World War II—but he was never again employed by the U.S. government.

Through all of his adventures and intrigues, Herbert Yardley was a dedicated poker player, spending hours at the table and (as he told it) virtually always winning. He would later attribute much of his success as a spy and code breaker to the card-playing skills he picked up as a teenager at Monty's Place, the only honest saloon and card room in his hometown of Worthington, Indiana. The eponymous owner of the joint took 16-year-old Yardley under his wing, teaching him the subtle and not-so-subtle arts of separating lesser players from their money and other worldly goods.

LAWYERS' POKER

In 1957, Yardley published *The Education of a Poker Player*, which is widely regarded as the first modern poker classic, setting out a series of axioms and principles for success. Each chapter begins with the story of a memorable hand—usually involving the preternatural wisdom of the great Monty—and concludes with a set of extremely specific rules for winning at five-card draw, five-card stud, and other games that were popular in the early twentieth century.

Most of Yardley's rules are ruthlessly categorical, often premised on the word "never," because above all else he was an advocate of tight play (which earned him the nickname "Old Adhesive"). "I do not believe in luck," Yardley explained, "only in the immutable law of averages." Thus, you should never bet unless you think you already have the best hand or the makings of one. As his mentor, Monty, put it:

> I am reminded of players who insist on "betting on the come"; that is, to bet that their next card will improve the hand. I have listened to their arguments and nodded in agreement, but I simply do not play that kind of poker unless the odds are in my favor. I figure the odds for every card I draw, and if the odds are not favorable, I fold. This doesn't sound very friendly. But what's friendly about poker? It's a cut-throat game at best.

Every contemporary poker writer owes a debt to Yardley, and most pay him homage even if they do not share his rigid commitment to supertight play. A. Alvarez, for example, summarizes Yardley's law: "Assume the worst, believe no one, and make your move only when you are certain either that your hand is unbeatable or that the odds are strongly in your favor." This is an ironclad system for playing against weak opponents, the sort who apparently were regularly cleaned out by Monty and his young protégé in small-town Indiana. Throughout his life, Yardley preferred low-stakes games, noting that the other players were inevitably looser ("simpletons," he often called them) and therefore more susceptible to his ultratight strategy.

Highly sophisticated players, however, will "recognize a 'rock' when they see him," as Alvarez observed, and fold their own hands whenever he bets strongly. While Yardley-coached players will seldom lose, given that they only bet on nearly sure things, they will seldom win big, at least in professional games, because no one with any sense will bet into them. Yardley was apparently content with not losing, even at the cost of limiting his winnings. Alvarez calls this "classical poker," the work of a purist writing for other purists.

Lawyers (not to mention clients) are usually far more risk averse than card players, especially at high stakes, so Yardley's classical approach is considerably more helpful in litigation than it is in poker: "I figure the odds for every card I draw," he said, "and if the odds are not favorable, I fold."

This rule, pure as it is, will carry you a long way in cross-examination, where it pays to scrutinize every question you are tempted to ask. Are the odds overwhelmingly positive for a favorable answer? Do you know how the witness is going to reply? In case of a surprise, can you impeach her with a prior statement? If so, go ahead with the question. If not, discard it and ask a different one. This technique will work with virtually any witness, although it may result in passing up some good stuff that cannot be nailed down in advance. Moreover, especially wily and well-prepared witnesses will be ready for this style of cross, coached by opposing counsel to refrain from arguing and to respond if possible in agreeable monosyllables. You will establish everything that can be fully documented, but not much more.

Even the most sophisticated witnesses, however, can often be baited into mistakes if the cross-examiner is willing to take a few calculated risks. In the renowned Scopes Monkey trial of 1925, Clarence Darrow took just that sort of chance when he called his adversary, William Jennings Bryan, to the witness stand.

John Scopes, a high school biology teacher in Dayton, Tennessee, was on trial for teaching the theory of evolution to his class, in violation of a state law that made it "unlawful for any teacher . . . to teach any theory that denies the story of the Divine Creation of man as taught in the Bible, and to teach instead that man has descended from a lower order of animals." The prosecution case had been the soul of simplicity. Bryan asked the court to take judicial notice of the Book of Genesis, and the judge complied. Then the prosecution called seven students who testified that Scopes had indeed taught them that man had descended from one-celled organisms. After establishing that Scopes was aware of the anti-evolution law, the prosecution rested.

The defense attempted to call a series of expert witnesses, both scientists and theologians, to testify about the validity of evolution and its compatibility with Christianity. The court, however, sustained the prosecution's objection, holding that the evidence regarding interpretation of the Bible was inadmissible, as experts could shed no light on whether Scopes had taught that man descended from a lower order of animals.

Frustrated, Darrow requested leave to examine Bryan himself as an expert on the Bible, a challenge that led, as the *New York Times* put it, to "the most amazing court scene in

Anglo-Saxon history." Bryan quickly agreed, showing more than a bit of disdain for Darrow's tactic: "It seems to me it would be too exacting to confine the defense to the facts; if they are not allowed to get away from the facts, what have they to deal with?"

The gauntlet thrown down, there was clearly no way that Bryan—the outstanding orator of his age and three times the Democratic party's candidate for president—would be a docile witness. But Darrow embraced the challenge, making no attempt to confine or control his answers.

At first, it seemed to go well for Bryan who was, after all, appearing before a friendly audience. Asked whether he believed that a whale had literally swallowed Jonah, Bryan confidently replied, "I believe in a God who can make a whale and can make a man and make both do what He pleases."

Well, mocked Darrow, would it be just as easy to believe that Jonah swallowed a whale?

"If the Bible said so," answered Bryan, adding pointedly that "the Bible doesn't make as extreme statements as evolutionists do."

Undeterred, Darrow repeatedly invited Bryan to expand on his literalist beliefs, showing that they were inconsistent with open scientific inquiry.

> QUESTION: Now Mr. Bryan, have you ever pondered what would have happened to the earth if it had stood still?
> ANSWER: No.
> Q: You have never investigated that subject?
> A: I don't think I have ever had the question asked.
> Q: Or ever thought of it?

A: I have been too busy on things that I thought
were of more importance than that.

Q: What do you think?

A: I do not think about things I don't think about.

Q: Do you think about the things you do think about?

Moving to another chapter and verse, Darrow continued to allow the witness complete latitude, while driving home his point that the Bible could not provide answers to every question.

Q: Mr. Bryan, do you believe that the first woman was Eve?

A: Yes.

Q: Do you believe she was literally made out of Adam's rib?

A: I do.

Q: Did you ever discover where Cain got his wife?

A: No sir; I leave the agnostics to hunt for her.

Q: The Bible says he got one, doesn't it. Were there other people on the earth at that time?

A: I cannot say.

Q: There were no others recorded, but Cain got a wife?

A: That is what the Bible says.

Again, Darrow posed a question that could be answered by science, but not by Bryan's literal interpretation of the Bible.

Q: I will read to you from the Bible: "And the Lord God said unto the serpent, because thou hast done this, thou art cursed above all cattle, and above every beast of the field; upon thy belly shalt thou go and dust shalt thou eat all the days of thy life." Do you think that is why the serpent is compelled to crawl upon its belly?

A: I believe that.

Q: Have you any idea how the snake went before that time?

Q: No, sir.

A: Do you know whether he walked on his tail or not?

Q: No sir. I have no way to know.

Finally, Bryan exploded. Confronted by a question about the rainbow and the flood, he lost his composure and began casting insults, just as Darrow hoped he would.

A: The only purpose Mr. Darrow has is to slur at the Bible, but I will answer his question. I will answer it all at once, and I have no objection in the world. I want the world to know that this man, who does not believe in God, is trying to use a court in Tennessee to slur at it, and while it will require time, I am willing to take it.

That was enough for the judge, who ended the examination and recessed the proceeding. It was enough for Darrow as well, who was more than satisfied with Bryan's answers. Rather than attempt to control the witness, as Yardley would surely have counseled, he had played out the line as far as possible. Banking on Bryan's ego and volatility, the bet paid off. The rest is history (and biology).

Even if you take the classic approach to poker, betting only when odds are favorable, you are bound to lose sooner or later. Sometimes, it's just a few hands, and sometimes you lose for the whole night (or longer). Sometimes, the losses are your own fault, and sometimes you can play perfectly and still go broke. The point is that losing is part of the game. No one is immune from it, and even the most skillful players cannot avoid it. In the long run, of course, there is no luck in poker, and the best players will eventually win. But as Alvarez explained, there is plenty of luck, both good and bad, in the short run, and "the short run is longer than most people know."

Managing losses, therefore, is one of the most important parts of the game. It is essential to keep them in perspective and, most of all, to prevent bad beats from influencing the way you play the next hand. It may seem counterintuitive, and it is certainly counterproductive, but there is a nearly universal tendency to play loosely in a misguided attempt to get even following a series of losses. Card players call it "going on tilt" or "steaming," and Andy Bellin describes it like this:

> After losing a big hand, a player bets and raises with garbage because he is steamed over the last game. Then he loses more, and a cycle begins. Once you tilt, there's almost no hope for recovery.

The right thing to do, of course, is to forget about the last hand while concentrating on the next round of cards. But it is not always easy. Puggy Pearson, the 1973 world champion, observed, "Losing is like smoking; it's habit forming." That is why, as 1978 world champion Bobby Baldwin pointed out:

> The mark of a top player is not how much he wins when he is winning but how he handles his losses. If you win for thirty days in a row, that makes no difference if on the thirty first you have a bad night, go crazy, and throw it all away. You can't survive that way. In this business, you have to be able to live with adversity.

The funny thing about steaming is that almost everyone is wary of it, but most players end up tilting anyhow. It is hard to recover from a breathtaking loss—when you made a foolish and costly mistake or, worse, when you were miraculously outdrawn on the river—while keeping your judgment intact. Almost inevitably, it seems, a process of rationalization sets in. You are due for better cards; the next hand is bound to be yours; your luck has to change sometime; the deck owes you a good hand; no one (meaning, your opponent) can be that lucky twice in a row. Of course, this is all nonsense. The cards have no memory, so each hand is an independent event. You can only win by playing the next hand correctly, on its own terms, not by attempting to redress the previous misfortune. Still, many card players manage to be oddly self-aware and self-delusional at the same time. "I pride myself on never tilting," says Andy Bellin, and yet "I tilt all the time."

If anything, lawyers are even more susceptible to steaming when things go wrong and more likely to rationalize bad behavior. Losing your temper in negotiation, berating a judge for a bad ruling, snarling at a surprisingly unhelpful witness—these are all examples of going on tilt, turning a momentary disadvantage into a potential debacle. Needless to say, most decent lawyers understand the need to maintain their composure, especially in court. Nonetheless, even the calmest among us will occasionally snap, and the less disciplined will throw outright tantrums, later rationalized (though never excused) with the self-justification that "it had to be said." Well, it almost certainly did not have to be said, especially if it was disrespectful, rude, crude, loud, or inconsiderate. Loutish outbursts might feel good (just like betting heavily on rag hands), but they almost never accomplish anything positive for your client.

But all of that is obvious. No one (well, almost no one) thinks it useful for lawyers to lose their tempers or behave badly. But there is also a more subtle lesson to be learned about steaming. Serious mistakes are more likely to happen when things are going wrong. Judgment becomes clouded when frustration sets in, and foolish temptations seem somehow irresistible. Perhaps the best example is the classic case of one question too many.

By now, everyone understands (at least on an intellectual level) the lurking danger in asking one question too many on cross-examination. Having painstakingly trapped a witness in an apparent contradiction or impossibility, the lawyer is not content to leave the finishing touch for final argument. Instead, he attempts to deliver the coup de grace, asking the ultimate question—only to be grievously surprised by the witness's perfectly logical explanation.

One famous version of the story is told about the young Abraham Lincoln, who was representing a defendant charged with biting off another man's nose. The prosecution called a single witness to the incident, who testified that Lincoln's client had indeed done the atrocious act. On cross-examination, Lincoln set out to show that the witness could not have seen all that he claimed.

> Q: The two men were fighting in the middle of a field?
>
> A: Yes.
>
> Q: You were birdwatching at the time?
>
> A: True.
>
> Q: Weren't the birds in the trees?
>
> A: They were.
>
> Q: And the trees were on the edge of the field?
>
> A: That is right.
>
> Q: So you were looking away from the middle of the field?
>
> A: I was.

So far, the cross-examination has gone swimmingly. The witness's head was turned completely away from the action. Rather than looking at the middle of the field, where the fight occurred, he was eyeing the birds in the surrounding trees. Enough! Stop! Mission accomplished! But no, the cross-examiner made the fatal error of asking another question.

> Q: Then how can you say that you saw my client bite off the other man's nose?
>
> A: Because I saw him spit it out.

Lesson learned. The extra question must never be asked; it leads only to catastrophe. The best cross-examinations will surely be dashed to pieces on the shoals of the unnecessary inquiry.

Well, not really. In reality, it is pretty easy to stop after getting a good answer, satisfied that you have done your job. It is much harder to stop after a bad one, when the urge to salvage something can occlude good sense and good judgment. So good cross-examinations are not the problem; they are seldom ruined by extra questions, because good cross-examiners—with their wits about them and their goals firmly in mind—do not usually give in to the temptation.

Then what about Abraham Lincoln, a great lawyer if ever there was one? It turns out that his cross-examination was not ruined by asking one question too many, because in fact he was laying a trap. His next set of questions asked the witness how he was able to see the events so well, given that the fight occurred at night. The witness answered, "I could see by the light of the full moon." That might have seemed like yet another question too many, but Lincoln went on to impeach his testimony by reading from the *Farmers' Almanac*. There was no moon at all that night.

Abraham Lincoln knew where he was going and maintained his composure, even when confronted by a witness who was clearly lying. He was unlikely to make a mistake precisely because he was not on tilt.

The real problem arises when a cross-examination is already on the rocks, and the lawyer is flailing for something—anything—that might save the day. In that situation, it is all too easy to forget the rules, especially when a witness has delivered a nasty surprise. Another historic case, the 1951 prosecution of Julius and Ethel Rosenberg for espionage, provides an example.

The Rosenbergs were accused of spying for the Soviet Union and delivering the secret of the atomic bomb to Russian agents. The principal witness against them was David Greenglass, Ethel's brother, who had worked as a low-level machinist on the Manhattan Project at Los Alamos, New Mexico. Greenglass testified that he had been enlisted in the Russian spy ring by his brother-in-law, whom he greatly admired. Fortuitously assigned to work at the facility where the bomb was being developed, Greenglass took notes and made sketches of the scientific processes, some of which he passed directly to Julius, and some of which he turned over to a courier named Harry Gold. In particular, Greenglass testified that he provided drawings of a top-secret high-explosive lens mold that was essential to building a bomb.

The defense lawyer, Emmanuel Bloch, faced the daunting task of cross-examining David Greenglass. Bloch was a friend and supporter of the Rosenbergs who labored mightily in their cause, but he was not much of a trial lawyer. From the beginning of the case, he was overwhelmed and outgunned by the highly experienced prosecution team, which included Irving Saypol, who had only recently secured the conviction of Alger Hiss. To make matters worse, the trial judge was hostile to the defense and, as was later discovered, the prosecution had withheld interview notes of their key witnesses.

Despite these obstacles, Bloch gamely attempted to undermine Greenglass's testimony. It did not go well from the beginning. The witness had already pled guilty to espionage, and he denied Bloch's assertion that his testimony was given in exchange for a lighter sentence. Greenglass admitted that he was a spy and a criminal, but he insisted that he had been recruited by Julius. In fact, Greenglass claimed, he had initially refused Julius's overtures, only to be persuaded by his repeated efforts.

Then, for a moment, the cross-examination seemed to make a bit of headway. Bloch was able to show that Greenglass had been a poor student, failing eight classes in high school, and that he had never studied calculus, thermodynamics, or nuclear physics. The implication, of course, was

that Greenglass would have been incapable of assembling
meaningful information about the technical aspects of the
bomb project. Bloch continued along this line, planning to
accentuate Greenglass's ignorance. Instead, he got a surprise.

Q: Do you know what an isotope is?
A: Yes.

Bloch should have known better than to follow up, but
he was not willing to accept a bad answer. Gambling on a
bad hand, he unwisely challenged the witness.

Q: What is it?
A: An isotope is an element having the same atomic
   structure, but having a different atomic weight.

That was already one question too many, but Bloch
was clearly annoyed at the ill-educated Greenglass's pre-
tentiousness. Unable to resist temptation, he made the bad
situation worse.

Q: Did you learn that in Los Alamos?
A: I picked it up here and there.
Q: Can you give me an instance?
A: A man came to me with a sketch—with a piece of
   material and said, "Machine it up so that I would
   have square corners, so I could lay out a lens;
   come over and pick it up." I would go over to his
   place. He was a scientist. I would say, "What is the
   idea?" He would tell me the idea.

Greenglass took advantage of Bloch's loose play to emphasize
his own involvement in fashioning the critical lens mold, as
well as his access to the information eventually turned over
to the Soviets.

Bloch made a crucial mistake because he was steaming. He was clearly angry at Greenglass—who had betrayed his own sister and brother-in-law, exposing them to the death penalty—for exaggerating his scientific knowledge. But just when a lawyer should have been the most cautious, he had plunged ahead, determined to recoup his losses by dragging something favorable out of Greenglass—no matter how bad the odds. In other words, tilt.

LESSON 10: *Desperate Times*

In poker, a feeling of desperation is usually a strong signal to quit for the night, before you go on "tilt" and make matters worse. The impulse to recoup losses in a hurry typically leads to recklessness and then disaster. It is usually far better simply to go home, calm down, and resume play later with more composure. In Doyle Brunson's words, "[I]t is important to learn how to go home a loser" because "nobody wins every day."

Lawyers, in contrast, seldom have the luxury of simply quitting, even for the night, when things go badly. The judge controls the trial, deciding on every adjournment, recess, and even bathroom breaks. A lawyer in dire straits usually has no choice but to soldier on, no matter how dismal the circumstances. Even in the pretrial phase, depositions and negotiations cannot be terminated at will; opposing counsel always has something to say about the matter and might be able to exact a price. Consequently, lawyers often find themselves in desperate times, searching, as the saying goes, for elusive desperate measures.

Clarence Darrow wasn't utterly desperate when he took his calculated risk in the Scopes trial, but only because he knew all along that he was destined to lose before the jury (composed almost entirely of local farmers and churchgoers). He still had to put on a case, however, in order to create some kind of record for the appellate court while simultaneously appealing to the broader public. The trial judge had thwarted his efforts to call recognized scientific experts to the stand, so his unorthodox response to the court's rulings—examining opposing counsel—was certainly a tactic of last resort.

There is one comparable situation for card players, when they cannot simply walk away from the table. In tournament poker, every player buys in for a set number of chips—in the World Series of Poker, it is $10,000—and plays until he goes broke. The field is constantly winnowed down to a final table of ten players, who are then eliminated one by one. The champion is the last player standing, the winner of all the chips. The catch, however, is that the antes and blinds (mandatory opening bets) constantly increase, eventually reaching five figures. A supertight player, following Yardley's strict directive to fold whenever the odds aren't favorable, will eventually go broke watching. Sooner or later, you have to play a hand before you bleed to death, even if your pocket cards are rags. Many of the most successful players prefer to do it sooner.

Doyle Brunson did just that at the 1976 World Series of Poker, when the final table was down to the last two players. Dealt 10♠ 2♥ before the flop, a questionable hand if there ever was one, he called Jesse Alto's initial bet. The flop came A-J-10, of different suits, giving Brunson a pair of tens. Alto, however, had A-J in the hole, giving him two pair. Brunson again called Alto's large bet, and a second deuce fell on the turn. This time Brunson bet aggressively (probably putting Alto on a pair of aces), and Alto called. Brunson caught another ten on the river, making his full house and winning his first WSOP championship.

Incredibly, Brunson won another championship the following year with the same hand. This time, Brunson held 10♠ 2♥ before the flop, while his remaining opponent, "Bones" Berland, held 8♥ 5♣. Although Brunson had the top card, Berland had a tenuous straight draw. The flop came 10♥ 5♦ 8♥, making Berland's two pair a big favorite over Brunson's tens. Knowing Brunson's reputation for aggressive play, Berland checked, which was probably a mistake. Brunson checked as well and got a free look at the turn which, as fate would have it, was another deuce. This time Berland went "all in," as he should have on the previous card when a large bet might have caused Brunson to fold. Now that Brunson held the top two pair, he called—and caught the third ten on the river. He didn't need the full house to win, but he got it, giving him his second consecutive WSOP victory with tens full of deuces. Ever since, the 10-2 combination has been called a "Doyle Brunson."

It is tempting to think about emulating the fancy maneuvers of the masters, especially when the heavens are falling and doom impends. Resist the temptation. It is unlikely that any contemporary judge would give you the latitude that Clarence Darrow finessed in Dayton, nor would a modern prosecutor willingly subject himself to such wide-ranging cross-examination. While some players may talk themselves into believing that the 10-2 combination is a lucky hand, wiser heads know better. Brunson himself, in a 2004 interview, confided, "I played the 10-2 many times after that. Let's just say I don't play it anymore."

Parlous times, when it looks as though there may be no tomorrow, call for courage and creativity. Alas, there is no set formula for pulling off the winning coup. The best advice is to play the hand you're dealt.

LESSON II: *Volatility*

Without cheating, there is no way to improve the quality of your cards, much less ensure that you will consistently out-draw your opponents. Winning at poker, therefore, depends almost entirely on making the most of the hands you're dealt—either by increasing your winnings on your good cards or by minimizing your losses when the poker gods frown. Between the two, it is much easier to minimize losses, given that you are in total control of your own bets. No one can make you call or raise; only you can decide how much money you are going to put in the pot. In contrast, you can only maximize your winnings when someone is willing to bet against you. For that reason, there is no necessary cor-relation between the quality of your hand and the value of the pot. If everyone else folds, even four aces are not worth more than the antes. In fact, you can often win more with a pocket pair, well hidden and correctly played, than with the top flush, when the other players can all figure out that you have the nuts.

One way to minimize losses is by avoiding small mis-takes, especially at the beginning of a hand. According to the modern study of chaos theory, there is an inevitable tendency for events to become more disordered and more unpredictable over time. Thus, you never have more control over your hand than at the very beginning. With each succeeding card, the hand becomes more volatile: You could fail to fill your straight, your opponent could flop a set, or virtually anything else could happen within the limits of the 2,598,960 possible five-card combinations in a 52-card deck.

You can reduce volatility in several different ways. The first, as we have already seen and as Herbert Yardley would strongly advise, is to fold immediately all but the most promising hands. It is usually a waste of money to call an early bet when you are holding rags or near-rags. Worse, you might subsequently be sucked into a couple of additional bets if your hand improves slightly, though not enough to win. Nothing eliminates volatility like tight play. But folding isn't the only answer to chaos theory. When circumstances allow, you might also be able to limp in when all of the other players have checked, allowing you to see the flop cheaply, or even for free.

Finally, and conversely, you can also decrease volatility by betting strongly on good cards. That approach will tend to drive out the drawing hands, meaning that they won't be around to beat you on the river.

The key is to understand that you have maximum command of your destiny at the beginning of each hand, but that control diminishes with every successive bet and card. A good, basic strategy, therefore, is either to avoid early commitments yourself (by folding or taking advantage of cheap cards) or to push your opponents into early commitments (by raising the bet before the flop). There are other, more-sophisticated tactics, of course, such as slow playing and bluffing, which we will address in later sections. For now, it

is sufficient to emphasize the crucial first decision: whether
to fold or raise.

Doyle Brunson believes that the optimum strategy is almost always either to fold (rags) or raise (with playable cards). "If you're going to call," he says, "you might as well bet" because that will increase the value of your hand. Brunson's logic is elegant in its simplicity. You seldom go wrong by folding, especially at the beginning of a hand, because that avoids risking money on losing cards. But *if* you intend to play, then raising rather than calling carries three advantages. First, raising creates two ways to win the hand—either with better cards or by causing everyone else to fold—in contrast to calling, which only allows you to win with the best hand. Additionally, raising increases the payoff on the hands that you do win. Finally, raising forces your opponents to make early decisions about their own hands, which in turn makes them susceptible to the risks of volatility.

There is no doubt that chaos theory also plays a part in the cross-examination of witnesses. The longer the examination continues, the more volatile it becomes. No matter how well prepared you are, no matter how much mastery you have displayed, an extended examination increases the risk that something will go wrong—the equivalent of allowing your opponent to outdraw you on the river. For that reason alone, seasoned trial lawyers almost always advise novices to keep their cross-examinations short. "Make no more than three points," it is often said. "Better yet, make only two; and best of all, make one telling point and sit down." It is an unusual lawyer who can exercise that amount of self-control, but the advice is sound. A shorter cross will make the examination more memorable, and importantly, it will reduce the chances of screwing up.

Perhaps even more significantly, the concept of volatility helps us to understand how essential it can be to assert control of a witness at the beginning of the cross-examination. When things start to go wrong, they tend to keep going wrong. Thus, it is far easier to contain a witness's answers early in the examination than it is to bring him back under control after he has gone astray. At that point, once the witness has launched a series of lengthy, nonresponsive answers, it can be costly or even impossible to get the examination back on track. Your efforts to limit his responses—"Just answer yes or no!"—may come off as blunt or badgering, damaging your credibility and alienating the jury. Worse, you may actually underscore the significance of the witness's volunteered answers. Worse yet, you may create the impression that you have something to hide. And worst of all, you might turn to the judge for help, only to be rebuffed or scolded: "I think the witness is being responsive, counsel. Ask another question, if you have one."

All of that can be avoided, or at least minimized, by following Doyle Brunson's advice either to fold or raise. In this case, folding means limiting the cross-examination to its bare essentials. Ask the minimum number of questions necessary to make the fewest possible fundamental points. Then sit down.

Raising, on the other hand, means establishing tight control from the outset, even if it does not seem important at the time. For example, some lawyers tend to ask open-ended questions on preliminary matters, thinking that it will make them seem friendlier and less confrontational. While that technique can be useful in depositions, where you want the witness in a chatty frame of mind, it can have the opposite effect on cross-examination, establishing a pattern of permissiveness that can be difficult to retract when the examination moves to more controverted material. It is far less risky to lead the witness from the very beginning (as gently as possible, of course), even on preliminary and uncontroversial matters.

Another effective technique—it might be called semi-impeachment—involves prominent use of the witness's deposition transcript or other prior statements. Make it clear from the outset that your cross-examination is pegged to the witness's own earlier words, quoting him if possible or perhaps reading from salient documents. Taught early that you have the goods, the witness will be more likely to agree with you, less likely to argue, and far less inclined to ramble or extemporize—especially once you have reminded him (again, gently) of your access to corrective measures.

To be sure, there will be situations where you want to take some risks or where efforts at early witness control may cause more problems than they solve. In that case, go ahead and start with open questions, or leave the deposition transcript in your briefcase. Every witness is different, and even Doyle Brunson has been known to call bets.

LESSON 12: *Sunk Costs*

Whether you are raising, calling, or folding, the size of the pot is crucial to your betting strategy because it determines the potential payoff ("pot odds"). You should be more willing to bet into a large pot than a small one, because there will be a bigger reward if you win. In other words, a big pot creates a greater expected value, meaning that you can afford to play a hand with a smaller chance of winning.

64

♦

It is equally important to understand, however, that the *origin* of the money in the pot is irrelevant. It does not matter how much money you have already bet because there is no such thing as protecting your investment. Rather, you should only consider the size of the next bet in relation to the amount of money you stand to win. An economist would call this the principle of sunk costs, meaning that only future costs (and potential profits) should drive your decisions.

David Sklansky, the son of a math professor and himself a former math major and actuary, explains that the money you have already contributed to the pot is of no consequence: "In truth, it is no longer yours. The moment you place your $1 ante in the pot, it belongs to the pot, not to you, and eventually to the winner of the hand." It is a common mistake for players to keep betting in the belief that they are already committed. In truth, that is just a way to throw good money after bad, making "a bad call because they called one or two bets on earlier rounds." As Sklansky points out, "[I]t is absolutely irrelevant whether you put the money in there or someone else did. It is the total amount, no part of which belongs to you any longer, that should determine how you play your hand." Anthony Holden puts it even more succinctly. "It is essential," he says, "to remember that money you have already paid into the pot is no longer yours; to defend it with more, in defiance of the odds, is an act of supreme folly."

And yet, novice poker players constantly defy this simple rule, justifying their behavior with careless aphorisms such as "it's too late to stop now" or, even more dangerously, "what the hell." That sort of loose play may be fun in a friendly game—and it would certainly cause Herbert Yardley to smile gratefully—but it is a sure way to lose money in the end. A bad bet is a bad bet (and a good bet is a good one), no matter how much money you have already contributed to the pot.

Lawyers, too, have a figurative tendency to throw good money after bad, which we see every time a cross-examiner doggedly pursues a dead-end line of questioning. Having been thwarted by a witness two or three times, the hapless lawyer insists on coming back for more, reasoning (if it can be called reasoning) that she must continue trying to make his investment pay off. That is backward thinking, of course, attempting to rescue the questions that have already been asked, rather than figuring the expected value of the questions yet to come. Is there a decent chance that the witness will actually change his tune, or will the examination just sink deeper into a pattern of denial and reproach?

Another variation on the sunk-costs phenomenon pops up in many depositions, when the deponent mildly resists the lawyer's line of questioning. Often the disagreement is over something as trivial as a word choice. But the lawyer digs in, unwilling to cede any ground whatsoever.

Q: Didn't that incident cause a complete rupture in your business relationship?

A: No, I wouldn't describe it that way.

Q: Are you telling me that everything was just fine?

A: Well, I would not call it a complete rupture.

Q: You haven't gotten any more orders, have you?

A: Not so far.

Q: Isn't that a rupture?

A: I hope it isn't.

Q: You haven't been told about any future orders?

A: No, we haven't.

Q: And yet, you still say there hasn't been a rupture?
A: I just wouldn't use that word.
Q: Why not?
A: It seems to me that a complete rupture means that things are over forever.
Q: The business relationship has never started up again, has it?
A: Not as of today.
Q: So it really was a complete rupture, wasn't it?

It is almost always a mistake to argue with a deponent, of course, but this is a particular kind of mistake. The lawyer has become possessive about her choice of words. Having thrown the idea of a "complete rupture" into the pot, she seems determined to defend it as the questioning proceeds. But for what reason? The additional questions are getting her nowhere. In fact, she is almost certainly impeding her own deposition—making the deponent tense and unhelpful, rather than cooperative and forthcoming. Perhaps the "complete rupture" question made sense the first time she asked it, but it quickly became a sunk cost, of no particular use to her. Thus, she should have quickly dropped it, concentrating on where the deposition was headed, rather than on where it had been.

Consider, then, an alternative line of questioning at the deposition, in which the lawyer is willing to abandon her commitment to the rupture and follow the witness's lead instead:

Q: Didn't that incident cause a complete rupture in your business relationship?
A: No, I wouldn't describe it that way.
Q: How would you describe it?

A: I guess I'd call it a serious breakdown in our relationship.

Q: That makes sense. Please tell me about the serious breakdown in your business relationship.

By adopting the witness's own description, the lawyer is clearly more likely to obtain useful information at the deposition. Yes, she had to give up on her original idea, but the reward was likely to be worth the cost. Only the next question matters; that last one is already gone.

LESSON 13: *Stakes Matter*

On one level, it might seem that poker skills and lawyering skills are pretty much transferable from one setting to another. If you can keep a poker face and disguise your hand in a $10 limit game, you ought to be able to do it at higher stakes as well. And if you can ask short, leading cross-examination questions in a run-of-the-mill contract case, you ought to be able to keep your questions equally tight in a serious felony prosecution or a catastrophic injury suit. After all, cards are cards and witnesses are witnesses—and everyone eventually wants to move up to the big time.

It turns out, however, that the stakes make a tremendous difference, and it can be a ruinous mistake—for at least two reasons—to move up before you are ready.

First, lower stakes mean less competition or, more precisely, less serious competition. As Herbert Yardley observed after he began playing beyond Monty's Place:

As I got farther from home I found the value of the bets smaller, the raises more frequent, and the games

wilder. I fashioned my method of play after long
study . . . and discovered that the smaller the stakes,
the wilder the game, the easier to win.

It stands to reason, of course, that lower stakes would
result in more bets and looser play, because the players themselves are less concerned about their losses, often willing to
throw a few more bucks into the pot for the sake of curiosity
or fun. That style of play is called "betting for action," rather
than for value. It is the kiss of death in professional poker,
but relatively harmless in casual games.

A determined player can almost always win in such a
game, ruthlessly exploiting the carefree attitude of his undis-
ciplined opponents. Yardley was evidently content to play
against simpletons, as he called them, taking advantage of
their weaknesses and raking in their money, though admittedly in fairly small amounts. Professionals refer to this as
"grinding," using supertight play in low-stakes games to
relieve amateurs of their mad money. Yardley, of course, was
an amateur himself. He was not interested in making a living
from his card skills, and he apparently never felt the need to
see how he would fair against stiffer competition.

Professionals, however, in both law and poker, typically
do feel the need to test themselves at the next level, either for
the sake of the challenge or simply to increase their profits.
And this brings us to the second peril inherent in raising the
stakes. Not only will you find yourself leaving the simpletons
behind, but you may also discover something—either good
or bad—about your own stamina and constitution under
pressure.

Andy Bellin wisely cautions that "one of the great mistakes you can make in poker is playing in a game where

the stakes are over your head. If you start thinking about the actual worth of all those clay chips, it knocks you off your game." It is easy to become scared when losses hurt too much, and fear is the enemy of rational calculation. Remember that the theory of expected value actually requires you to play potentially losing hands (so long as the pot odds justify the bet). Well, that can be a pretty tough strategy to maintain when the losses turn your knees to jelly. That is why A. Alvarez calls the Las Vegas poker tables "the graveyards of hometown champs." Successful card players from all over the United States come to Vegas "to test their skills," he says, but "nearly all of them go home broke."

While many people simply buckle under extreme pressure, for some players (and lawyers) it acts as a stimulus. Far from being intimidated, the high stakes actually help to concentrate their thinking by making the games more worthwhile. Alvarez, among others, was impressed by the nonchalance of the champions:

> The casualness and imperturbability with which that elite handles huge sums of money is beyond ordinary understanding. It is a question not just of a different level of skill but of a different ordering of reality.

A different ordering of reality, indeed. At the very highest stakes, say no-limit Texas Hold'em or bet-the-company litigation, courage becomes an essential element of strategy. When the slightest mistake can mean disaster, even otherwise simple decisions can be paralyzing. Again, Alvarez provides us with an elegant aphorism: "Imagination starts where logic falters, and transforms reality for its own ends." But only the truly bravehearted are willing to trust their imaginations at the most precarious moments.

Card players have the excuse that they are gambling with their own money. If they want to take a chance by raising the stakes, well, it is their chance to take. Maybe they will win, or maybe they will go broke, but no one else (except their creditors and families) will have to bear the consequences.

Lawyers have no such leeway. Clients suffer when attorneys overestimate their skills or underestimate the competition. It can be tempting to move to the big time, by accepting a court appointment, for example, or by filing an immense class action. But it makes far more sense, and it is far more responsible, to move forward incrementally with increasingly complex matters.

Card players have one further unique method of dealing with pressure. They play for chips, not cash. The use of poker chips allows players to suspend their doubts and misgivings during the game (or maybe fools them into it), temporarily easing the fear of losing by obscuring the difference between high stakes and small change. "Chips are like a bag of beans," says Alvarez, "they have a relative value and are worthless until the game is over. That is the only attitude you can have in high-stakes poker." Or, as Andy Bellin put it:

> If gamblers had to count out ten hundred dollar bills every time they lost $1000, a lot less money would be wagered. But the chips are meaningless. They are more like Lego blocks than money. When you lose a $200 pot, that's barely twenty chips. You hardly notice them gone from your stack. And at the end of the game, if you've lost all your money, you don't have to pay a thing. You've already cashed in. So all you have to do is walk away from the table.

Chips are so essential to poker games that card players have an oft-repeated saying (frequently attributed to a mythical New Yorker named Big Julie): The person who invented gambling was smart, but the person who invented chips was a genius.

Lawyers would do well to create their own saying: In litigation, there are no chips, but there are clients.

CLUBS *Controlling the Opposition*

The foundation of good poker is self-control, making only wise bets when you are likely to win and folding when the odds are unfavorable. But disciplined play will carry you only so far. The key to greater success is influencing the behavior of your opponents—making them fold when they might beat you and inducing them to keep betting when they are sure to lose. This ability separates the good players from the stars. Likewise in law, it is important to control witnesses' testimony, making sure that you get precisely the answers you need. Better yet, you might even be able to lure your adversaries into ruinous mistakes. An excellent example of the latter occurred during the O. J. Simpson trial, when the late Johnnie Cochran outmaneuvered prosecutor Christopher Darden.

It should have been a moment of high drama for the prosecution, as Darden laid the foundation for admission of the infamous "bloody gloves," one of which was recovered at the crime scene while the other was found at Simpson's home. A buyer for Bloomingdale's department store in New York had testified that Nicole Brown Simpson purchased an identical pair of gloves—brown leather Aris Isotoner lights, men's extra large, with cashmere lining—about five years earlier, presumably as a gift for her husband. Then Richard Rubin, a former vice president of Aris Isotoner, testified that only 300 pairs of such gloves had been manufactured, specially for Bloomingdale's, of which only about 240 had been sold.

At that point, Darden asked Simpson to step forward and try on the gloves. A good fit would have been visually devastating to the defense, as it was already established that they were stained by the blood of both victims. Imagine the compelling drama, if O. J. Simpson, in full view of the jury, had simply slipped his hands into the gloves that admittedly held the murder weapon. It would have been the equivalent of placing him at the crime scene.

The court solicited a defense objection, but Cochran declined the invitation without hesitation.

Darden handed Simpson the right-hand glove, which had been found near the bodies of Nicole Simpson and Ron Goldman. As the jury watched transfixed, the defendant slid his hand partway into the glove and began to tug. "Too tight, too tight," he muttered, continuing to pull at it. He eventually managed to squeeze most of his hand into it, but it was obvious to everyone in the courtroom that the glove was too snug. Believing that Simpson was faking the poor fit, Darden asked for an instruction that he "straighten his fingers and put them in the gloves as one would normally put them in the glove." The judge denied the request.

Most observers believe that the prosecution's glove fiasco was the turning point in the case—allowing Simpson to "testify" without taking the stand and making conviction nearly impossible. "It should have been a golden moment, and it backfired," said trial analyst Laurie Levinson.

Had defense counsel simply been lucky that Darden impulsively tried the in-court experiment? Not at all. The fateful demonstration was actually the result of an elaborate setup, in which the prosecution was successfully baited into a historic blunder.

Cochran had realized much earlier that the gloves could never be made to fit his client—for at least two reasons. First, he knew that Simpson would first have to put on a pair of latex surgical gloves to prevent contamination of the evidence. And even more significantly, he had taken advantage of a previous cross-examination (of the Bloomingdale's buyer) to try the gloves on himself. "Do these run small?" he asked the witness. "They stretch," she replied. That was enough for Cochran, since he knew full well that his client, on trial for his life, would never voluntarily stretch the skin-tight gloves.

After that, it was just a matter of getting the prosecutors to fall into the trap. The defense took advantage of a break in the proceedings to throw down the gauntlet. According to Cochran's memoir, his co-counsel F. Lee Bailey taunted the young prosecutor: "If you had any nuts at all," Bailey said, "you'd make O. J. try on that glove. If you don't have him try on the glove, we will." For whatever reason, recklessness or pride, Darden accepted the challenge, literally betting the case that he could show a winning hand.[1]

The prosecution attempted to recover after Simpson's dramatic display. Darden returned to the direct examina-

---

[1] Darden's own memoir tells a far different story, with no reference to provocation by Bailey, although the result is the same.

tion of Rubin, establishing that the latex gloves could have impeded the fit, that the crime-scene gloves could have shrunk in the course of testing, and that, in any event, the Aris Isotoner lights were intended to be skintight, "not baggy" like ordinary gloves. Those were decent arguments, but the case was already lost. As everyone knows, Johnnie Cochran had a stronger card to play: "If the gloves don't fit, you must acquit."

Opposing lawyers and witnesses can be controlled, or at least influenced, by any number of tactics and ploys, ranging from provocation to cajolery to sly manipulation. And this is true at every stage of law practice: pleading, negotiation, discovery, and trial. As the following lessons show, poker players have much to offer when it comes to mastering these techniques.

LESSON 1: *Fundamentalism*

Before he ever tried to lure Christopher Darden to disaster, Johnnie Cochran assured himself that the bloody gloves could never be slipped successfully onto his client's hands. Paying close attention to the fundamentals of advocacy, he had actually examined the necessary latex liners during an earlier recess, and his cross-examination of the Blooming-dale's buyer confirmed that the gloves "ran small." With all of the pieces in place, he was in a good position to take full advantage of the prosecutor's rash decision.

A winning card player strives to do the same thing, betting only in situations that offer positive expectations. But while she can precisely figure the odds of filling or improving her own hand, her opponent's hand remains partially, and therefore crucially, unknown. If she knew all of his cards, of course, she could always make the mathematically correct play, ensuring a profit at the end of the game (and by concealing her own hand, she could force her opponent into errors by keeping him in the dark). The art of poker, therefore, lies in filling the gaps in the incomplete information to allow you to make good decisions, while simultaneously preventing your opponents from learning any more than you want them to know about your own hand.

This leads to David Sklansky's perceptive "fundamental theorem of poker":

> Every time you play a hand differently from the way you would have played it if you could see all your opponents' cards, they gain; and every time you play your hand the same way you would have played it if you could see all their cards, they lose. Conversely, every time opponents play their hands differently from the way they would have if they could see all your cards, you gain; and every time they play their hands the same way they would have played if they could see all your cards, you lose.

Thus, you want to base your own decisions on valid information about your adversaries, while depriving them of any opportunity to do the same. The key to this process is the interpretation of betting behavior. You want to read your opponents' bets as accurately as possible and, perhaps more important, you want to make your own betting behavior inscrutable.

In poker, a bet is both an action and a signal. The action consists of adding to, matching, or declining to match the addition of a certain amount of money to the pot. That act

also provides information about your level of confidence in
your hand—a signal about your strength and intentions. Ide-
ally, following Sklansky's fundamental theorem, you would
want to accomplish two objectives with each bet. First, you
would want to make the "correct" move in light of your
opponent's cards: folding if she has you beaten, increasing
the pot if you are likely to win. Equally important, you would
want your bet, in its signaling capacity, to induce your opponent to make an incorrect move: calling when she is sure to
lose, folding if she holds winners.

In litigation, each "play" has a similar dual character. A
litigation move has an instrumental purpose: presenting a
motion to the court, objecting to a document demand, asking a deposition question. Each act also includes a signal.
For example, resistance to a document request has the per-
formative effect of denying (or at least delaying) discovery to
the other side. As a signal, it also conveys information, however ambiguously or unintentionally. Perhaps the resistance
means that you are planning to play hardball, whatever the
cost. Perhaps you are hiding a smoking gun. Perhaps you are
exploiting access to an unlimited litigation budget by running up the tab. No matter what the case, it is inevitable that
your opponent will attach an extrinsic meaning to some or
all of your maneuvers. Consequently, you will be most successful if you can influence and predict your opponent's
interpretation, and therefore reaction, to each signal.

This phenomenon can be seen most clearly in negotiation and settlement. Every offer, including the first, is an act
of independent legal significance. It can be accepted, creating a binding contract and thereby ending the negotiation.
More realistically, early offers act as signals, partially revealing but not fully disclosing your true bottom line. The art of

negotiation lies in correctly reading your adversary's intentions ("I can tell he will go higher") while obscuring your own ("final offer"). More complex negotiations will include throwaways and sweeteners, items of little importance to you that are either withheld or proffered to gain concessions from the other side. Again, success depends upon creating the impression that you hold these items dearly, even if you do not. Thus, you will give away the least while influencing your adversary to offer the most.

LESSON 2: *Know Why You Are Betting*

It may seem obvious that you bet in poker, or anywhere else, because you think you will win. But it is not nearly that simple; each bet also has a secondary purpose as a motivator, intentionally conveying a fragment of information to the opposition, in the hope that they will respond to your benefit. According to Bellin:

> To simplify a very complicated concept, there are basically two purposes to betting. The first is fairly self-evident. You want other people's money. Therefore, if you genuinely believe that your hand is the best, you want to bet and raise so you can increase the amount of money contained within the pot.
>
> The other reason you bet—and raise—is to narrow the field. You eliminate some, or all, of the competition and therefore have a better chance of winning. It's important to remember that these two concepts are often counterproductive. The more people you play against, the more money there is at stake. But at the

same time, the more people participating in a hand, the less likely it is that you'll hold the winning hand.

Expanding on this concept, David Sklansky identifies four basic reasons for betting, only the first of which (to get more money in the pot when you have the best hand) is purely instrumental. The other reasons, to varying degrees, are meant to influence the opposition: driving out other players, bluffing, and gaining information from the others' responses.

In other words, you bet for the purpose of influencing the other players. Your bets can either bring money into the pot (when other players call) or keep money out of the pot (when other players fold). Players who fold do not pay you, but they cannot beat you. Players contribute money to the pot when they call, but they may end up outdrawing you and taking it for themselves.

How does one resolve the betting dilemma? Should you bet aggressively and drive players out, even at the cost of a much smaller pot? Or is it preferable to bet cautiously, or not at all, thereby encouraging others to stick around and raise the stakes? As you might guess, there is no single correct answer. Rather, the best approach depends upon an intricate assessment of both the cards and your opponents' attitudes.

In brief, the optimum strategy is to misrepresent your hand, thereby causing your opponents to play their hands incorrectly. The better your cards, the less aggressively you bet. If your hand is unbeatable (the nuts, in poker slang), you do everything you can to indicate weakness, "slow playing" in the hope that the second-best hand will begin raising aggressively. When you do bet or raise, you will want it to look like a bluff, encouraging inferior, though perhaps pretty good, hands to raise back. If you hold a weaker hand—good enough to keep playing, but not a sure winner—you will probably show strength, betting and raising to drive out the competition. This is especially true when your hand is incomplete but potentially powerful, say four cards to a flush or an open-ended straight. The chances of filling your hand may be pretty good, but there are never any guarantees. Consequently, you may play as though you have already made your hand, encouraging the competition to fold. This is called semi-bluffing, since you can win either by forcing everyone else out or by actually drawing the winning card.

The point is that winning players evaluate the consequences of each bet, measuring it against a complex matrix of possible results. They are betting not only on the value of the cards, but also on their opponents' predicted reactions. The best players are able to vary their technique to avoid predictability—sometimes they play strong hands strongly (which makes their subsequent bluffs more convincing); sometimes they intentionally fold winners (to encourage other players to bluff with weak hands, planning to call them later, in larger pots).

With that in mind, let us now turn to cross-examination. All of the handbooks caution brevity, advising lawyers to cross-examine only on sure points, and as few of those as feasible. And again, too many lawyers persist in conducting long, searching, counterproductive cross-examinations. Why do they do this? Because they don't know why they are betting.

The purpose of cross-examination is not to gather information, but rather to tell a story. The goal of a good cross-examination is to extract useful answers from a witness who is frequently uncooperative. In essence, the lawyer wants to be the narrator, explaining her client's case, with the witness merely providing the necessary affirmation of the lawyer's points. Witnesses typically resist. Having been called by the opposing party, they are often resentful or wary of the cross-examiner, if not genuinely biased or hostile.

In essence, then, every cross-examination question actually represents a bet. The lawyer wagers her control of the witness (and her personal credibility) against the chance of a favorable answer. Some questions are low risk, designed to encourage cooperation and keep the witness in play. Aggressive questioning raises the stakes, increasing the possibility that the examination will backfire. The witness may clam up or become recalcitrant; worse, the jury might be alienated by the attorney's browbeating.

As in poker, success depends upon an accurate assessment of the likely response. Some witnesses are naturally cooperative and can easily be led wherever counsel wants to take them. Some witnesses have to be "disciplined" by tough questioning, while others will simply be intimidated into sympathy-engendering silence.

Thus, every question has both a potential positive value (in terms of getting an answer), as well as a potential negative cost (silencing the witness, incurring the judge or jury's anger). The values, however, are not constant. They vary from witness to witness and even as a single cross-examination progresses.

This underscores the utility of Bellin's insight. All raises are not the same. Just as there are multiple *contradictory purposes* for betting, there are multiple *contradictory techniques* for cross-examination. The lawyer's challenge is to match the technique to the occasion.

Imagine, for example, that a witness's direct examination has changed a small but relatively important detail from his deposition testimony. Does the lawyer want to impeach him? And if so, when? This decision can be approached by recalling the default rule in poker betting: Show strength when holding a weak hand, bet slowly when holding great cards.

Thus, if the lawyer believes that the witness has little to add to the case on cross-examination (weak cards), she may want to impeach the witness sharply and immediately. On the other hand, if the witness is likely to be useful to the lawyer's own case (strong cards), the impeachment may cost more than it delivers, by essentially driving the witness out of the game.

Even when the impeachment is absolutely essential, counsel must still decide where to situate it in the cross-examination. An early impeachment, like a large opening bet, is likely to have the most powerful impact. It might succeed brilliantly, disciplining the witness into eager compliance. But it is also more likely to boomerang in any of several ways. It might generate sympathy for a witness who, at the outset of the examination, does not yet seem to deserve harsh treatment. It might provoke an otherwise tractable witness to become unnecessarily contentious. Worst, it might fail with a thud, putting the lawyer on the defensive and tipping the scales in favor of the witness for the balance of the cross-examination.

The trial advocacy books (mine included) all caution against impeaching witnesses unnecessarily. Poker theory provides an additional way to quantify the decision. You do not impeach a witness just because you can, in the same way that you do not bet strongly simply because you hold

good cards. Sometimes, "slow playing" is the right way to
go: Allow the witness to remain uncontradicted, the better
to keep her in play.

LESSON 3: *Slow Playing*

Slow playing is a betting strategy—or rather, a nonbetting
strategy—that is intended to forestall your opponents from
folding their losing hands. When you hold the nuts, or something close to it, a monster bet may cause most or all of the
other players to throw away ("muck") their hands, meaning
that you will win a small pot despite your great cards. So
instead of betting heavily on the early rounds, you can slow
play—simply checking or calling others' raises, keeping them
in the game and building up the pot. Successful slow playing requires that you give nothing away about the strength
of your hand, while encouraging your opponents to believe
that their hands are likely to win.

Poker theorist David Sklansky identifies a set of conditions for successful slow playing. First, and most obviously,
you must have a very strong hand. Slow playing basically
allows your opponents to draw free cards, meaning that they
can improve their own hands at little cost. Therefore, you
must be all but certain that you can beat them even if they
fill their hands, or else slow playing is just too risky. Then
again, you want those free cards to improve your opponents'
hands, so that they will keep betting to the river. The best
scenario is when someone else holds a strong second-best
hand, as that will draw the most money into the pot. Finally,
you must be fairly sure that you would actually drive other
players out of the game if you bet your own hand aggres-

sively. If you think they would call your raises, rather than fold, then slow playing will cost you money by depressing the value of the pot.

Yardley's mentor, Monty, had slow playing down to a science. In one memorable hand, Monty went head to head with Slocum, the banker's son and one of the richest men in town, in a game of five-card stud (one down, four up). There was a bet of only $5 on the first round, but the betting jumped to life on the third card. Slocum was showing 7 A, and Monty was high with a pair of sevens on the board. Monty made a small bet of $10, and Slocum raised $20, which Monty called.

Yardley was puzzled. Slocum was clearly representing a pair of aces, which would ordinarily have caused the super-tight Monty to fold a pair of sevens. What was the hole card that caused Monty to call the bet?

Slocum drew a ten on the fourth card, giving him ? 7 A 10. Monty's card was a five, making ? 7 7 5. Again, Monty checked his pair, and this time Slocum bet $50. When Monty called the bet, Yardley became sure that his hole card was a seven, giving him three of a kind. Monty would never have backed a pair of sevens that far against an obvious pair of aces. He was clearly playing possum to keep Slocum in the game.

On the fifth and final card, Slocum caught another ten, making ? 7 A 10 10. Monty drew a queen, for ? 7 7 5 Q. Slocum's second ten looked dangerous, but in fact two of the earlier players had fold tens—so Slocum did not have trips. He did have aces over tens, of course, so he bet $100 on his two pair.

Monty raised $1,500. Had he given up the slow play? Not exactly. When Monty drew the queen on the last card, he realized that he could represent his own two pair—queens over sevens—so the huge raise did not give away his true hand. That is exactly how Slocum read the situation. Believing that his aces up were still good, he took the bait and called the bet.

Monty's slow play was perfect. He concealed his own strength in the early rounds, which was impressive enough. The really great move, however, came at the end, when he successfully represented a decent-but-not-great hand. That explained his immense raise, while continuing to suck Slocum into the pot. Slocum figured out that Monty was holding pretty good cards, but he did not realize how good until it was too late.

Lawyers often slow play on cross-examination, lulling witnesses into a false sense of security while setting them up for the kill. But no lawyer ever slow played a more consequential hand than Philip Beck, in a case that eventually determined the presidency of the United States.

Following the 2000 presidential election, the entire country watched in fascination as the ballots in Florida were counted and recounted. After weeks of uncertainty, Republican state officials certified George W. Bush as the winner, by about 500 votes out of more than 5 million cast, prompting Al Gore to challenge the election in court. A key issue in the lawsuit was the reliability of the punch-card voting machines that had been used in many heavily Democratic counties. The Gore campaign alleged that flaws in the equipment resulted in thousands of so-called undervotes, ballots that had been duly cast but not tallied. The Gore campaign wanted a hand recount of all of the ballots in certain designated counties. The Bush campaign countered that the machines had worked properly and that no further recount was necessary.

Working frenetically on a severely truncated schedule, each side located expert witnesses and began preparing for trial. The Democrats disclosed Dr. Nicholas Hentgartner of Yale University as an expert on statistics and demography. According to Hentgartner, the large number of undervotes in Palm Beach County was so anomalous that it could only have been caused by machine malfunctions, rather than random voter error. His opinion, based on an analysis of both 1998 and 2000 voting patterns in Palm Beach County, strongly supported the Democrats' case for a hand recount.

The Republicans were represented by Philip Beck of Chicago's Bartlit, Beck, Herman, Palenchar, & Scott. In the course of its pretrial investigation, the Bush team had discovered a mistake in an affidavit that Hentgartner had prepared at an earlier stage of the case. The expert had based his opinion about the prevalence of undervotes on certain erroneous assumptions about the design of the 1998 Palm Beach ballot. This mistake completely undermined Hentgartner's opinion, because it demonstrated that he relied on the 1998 ballots without ever having seen one. Beck knew that the actual 1998 ballot would be devastating to Hentgartner on cross-examination, but first there would be a 90-minute discovery deposition.

Some lawyers would have confronted Hentgartner with his error at the first opportunity, hoping to unnerve him before he testified at trial. Beck, however, decided to slow play. The mistaken affidavit was Beck's ace in the hole, and he had no intention of revealing it through aggressive questioning. Using the ballot reference during the deposition would only have allowed the Democrats to "fold" their hand, giving them numerous options. They might have found another expert to replace Hentgartner; they could have proceeded without an expert statistician; or, forewarned, they could have "pulled the stinger" by addressing the mistake during Hentgartner's direct examination.

Beck, of course, wanted Hentgartner to testify expansively, knowing that his overconfidence would end up damaging the Democrats' case. He therefore assigned the deposition to a young colleague, a former U.S. Supreme Court clerk, with the stern instruction that he should "not ask a single intelligent question."

As legend has it, Beck said, "If you ask one decent question, you're fired." The lawyer took his orders to heart and proceeded to interrogate Hentgartner about nothing more substantive than the textbooks he used in his classes at Yale. After 90 minutes of desultory inquiries, the deposition came to a merciful end. The young lawyer had done his job. The Democrats no doubt suspected that something was afoot, but they did not know just how good Beck's cards really were.

At trial, Hentgartner confidently testified on direct examination, explaining his comparison of the 1998 and 2000 voting patterns in Palm Beach County. Cross-examination was a different story. Beck asked the witness whether he had ever studied the 1998 ballot design.

"Not closely," answered Hentgartner.

"In fact," continued Beck, brandishing the ballot, which the Gore lawyers evidently had never seen, "you never actually examined it at all."

With that, Hentgartner's testimony foundered. The basis for his opinion, not to mention Al Gore's case for the presidency, was thoroughly undermined when Philip Beck finally played his cards.

Slow playing works by concealing great cards, representing your hand as weaker than it is. The complementary tactic is bluffing, representing far better cards than you really hold.

LESSON 4: *Bluffing*

Bluffing may well be the most misunderstood aspect of poker. The popular image of the bluffer is someone who makes a practice of betting massively on rag hands, using bluster and braggadocio to bully other players—fearful of calling the bluff—out of the pot. In this scenario, bluffing is the signature style of certain players, who invariably attempt to win by domination.

Nearly every aspect of that description, however, is inaccurate. The most artful bluffing is a means of distraction, not domination. It is part of a comprehensive, long-term strategy employed to prevent other players from ever accurately gauging the strength of any particular hand. It is fairly evident that bluffing is most successful when it is indistinguishable from betting for value: You want your opponents to think you have the nuts even when you don't; they fold their hands, and your bluff carries the day. The corollary is equally important if somewhat less obvious: Betting for value is most effective when it is indistinguishable from bluffing.

The surest way to win money in poker is to convince other players to bet against you when you hold the better hand, the precise opposite of bluffing. Not being idiots, most players will not do this intentionally; they have to be lured into it. Bellin explains it this way:

In its most rudimentary form, poker is a game where one player says, I am willing to bet that my hand is better than yours. It takes another player to doubt that, to assume that *his* hand is actually the best, for the game to continue. If you play . . . very mechanically, where the amount you are willing to wager increases proportionately with the strength of your hand—then as a player, you become extremely predictable. Other players would be able to accurately guess the strength of your hand as soon as you made a wager. The only time you would ever have a bet called (and possibly make more money than the ante) is when you actually hold the weaker hand, which makes for a really long night.

Players who raise only when they cannot lose will quickly find themselves with no callers, resulting in the paradox that the very best cards will win the smallest pots. Effective play, therefore, requires that opposing players always doubt your intentions. They have to wonder whether you are betting from strength or from weakness. When you play your cards right, they will guess wrong—folding when they should call and calling when they should fold.

The necessity of varying your play virtually requires occasional bluffing, or representing much greater strength than your actual cards justify. Game theorists John von Neumann and Oskar Morgenstern, in their classic academic analysis of poker, conclude that bluffing is an essential component of optimum strategy because it conveys "confusing information" to the opposition.

The creation of doubt results in four possible outcomes, three of which produce positive profits. If you are betting from strength and your opponent folds, you will win a relatively small pot. If you are betting from strength and your opponent calls, you will win even more. If you are bluffing and your opponent folds, you win. Finally, if you are bluffing and your opponent calls, you lose. Or do you?

Bellin's insight is that there can be a great strategic value to occasionally getting caught: It demonstrates that "you have the capacity to bluff. It's like an advertising budget." Since you frequently want other players to think that you might be bluffing (thus encouraging them to bet against your best cards), they have to see that you actually do it once in a while. And the more often you are caught, the more often they will call your bets, and even raise them. The trick, of course, is to strike the right balance, so that your play will always come as a surprise, and the opposing players will always be off-guard.

In litigation, there is no precise parallel to bluffing, since the opposing side rarely simply folds. What's more, there is seldom an advantage to be gained by inducing the opposition to continue playing; it is usually much better to learn their position as early as possible.

Nonetheless, there is a reasonable analogy in the process of pretrial negotiation, especially as it is played out in the course of discovery. While the ostensible purpose of discovery is to exchange information in preparation for trial, in reality it is much more a settlement dance, where the parties bluff and posture about the strength of their respective cases (and witnesses) in order to extract the maximum offer from the other side. Discovery tactics can be either aggressive (resisting disclosure) or accommodating (volunteering information). Lawyers who invariably follow a single approach become predictable and therefore lose the ability to influence their opponents' settlement position.

For example, some attorneys are vigorous, nearly to the point of obstructionism, in defending depositions. Lawyers who invariably follow this approach quickly develop reputations as blusterers, and no one takes them seriously. Thus, their own constancy renders the technique ineffective. But what happens when such a lawyer uncharacteristically encourages his own witness to begin volunteering during a deposition? The departure from the norm may become freighted with meaning, suggesting that the lawyer has exceptional confidence in both the witness and the case, which might in turn cause the opposing side to reconsider its view of settlement.

Then again, the unexpected turn toward cooperation might be, in effect, a bluff—intended only to convey a contrived attitude of confidence. Opposing counsel, however, will have no way of measuring the true meaning of counsel's move, but will surely have to wonder what he is up to. Sometimes, that uncertainty may lead to reevaluation and even self-doubt.

Bellin draws the poker player's conclusion that there is no such thing as an unsuccessful bluff. "If it works, fantastic, you win the pot." And if it doesn't, you have at least laid the groundwork for enhancing your winnings in the future.

This principle has to be amended for lawyers. Let's say, there are no unsuccessful surprises, and they don't all have to be flat-out bluffs. The next two lessons show the value of two more surprise techniques: reverse bluffing and semi-bluffing.

LESSON 5: *Reverse Bluffing*

A. Alvarez calls Jack Straus "the master of the withering bluff and a man with a reputation for total fearlessness." Some of Straus's bluffs have been so impressive that the rail birds actually burst into applause, awed by his willingness to bet huge amounts of money on the possibility that his opponents will lose their nerve. It takes a lifetime, or at least a good many years, to develop that sort of reputation, and it cannot be done by bluffing alone. The point is that Jack Straus successfully disguises his hand, representing cards that he might or might not actually hold. And you have to pay to find out.

At a high-stakes side game during the 1981 World Series of Poker, Alvarez watched Straus use his reputation to stunning advantage. In addition to Straus, the game involved some of the biggest names in poker—Doyle Brunson, Puggy Pearson, Crandall Addington, and Jesse Alto—with a buy-in of $50,000. After a few hours of unexciting play, Alto modestly raised a hand before the flop. Straus reraised, Alto called, and everyone else folded.

The flop came K 10 8, unsuited. Alto, who had K 8 in the hole, checked to Straus, hoping to trap him by slow playing his two pair. Straus bet $1,000, a middling amount by the standards of the game. Alto quickly reraised $5,000, certain that his tactic had worked. Straus paused and stared, looking intently at his opponent. Then he shoved a huge stack of chips into the pot, raising $30,000.

Now it was time for Alto to do the thinking. Could Straus be holding his own two pair, or even three of a kind? Did the flop give him four cards to an open-ended straight (which would make it a semi-bluff; more on that later), or was he bluffing all the way? The pot odds favored folding—he would be risking $30,000 with only $12,000 already in the pot—but maybe that was just the calculation Straus was counting on, hoping to steal Alto's early bets. After long minutes without moving or speaking, Alto pushed his whole stack of chips into the pot. Straus's $30,000 had set him "all in," so there would be no further betting on the hand.

Alto flipped over his king and eight, showing his two pair. Straus nodded appreciatively and flipped over his own hole cards: a pocket pair of tens, giving him a set of three. With two cards to come, Alto needed another king to beat him. The dealer dealt a seven on the turn and a four on the river, giving Straus the pot.

Of course, that was far from a bluff. Straus's pocket pair looked good from the beginning, and he was a heavy favorite to win when he flopped the third ten. The real challenge for Straus was building up the pot by getting Alto to call his heavy bet. You might think of it as a bit of tactical jujitsu. He wanted Alto to think he was bluffing, or at least chasing, when he was really holding great cards. How did Straus do it? Alvarez describes it this way:

> In the previous hour, Straus had twice bet in precisely the same pattern, but with weaker cards; both times, Alto had called him and won. The only difference was that the sums involved had been much smaller—a couple of thousand rather than tens of thousands. I had watched those two earlier hands uncomprehending, for it seemed—even to an outsider and relative novice like me—that Straus was betting on losing cards.
>
> I was wrong, of course. Straus had been setting Alto up for the kill, raising his confidence, lulling him

into the belief that he, Straus, was playing loosely, so that when his moment came he could make the same ploy with a monster hand and Alto would call him. The two losing hands were investments that finally yielded a disproportionate return—$8,000 to make $40,000.

It can take time and patience, and sometimes a significant investment, to influence someone as capable as Jesse Alto, who has finished as high as second in the World Series of Poker. Straus's play was all the more impressive because it was part of a long-term strategy, designed to take advantage of his opponent's weaknesses. Knowing that he was unlikely to intimidate Alto into folding a good hand, he took exactly the opposite approach, figuring out a way to entice his opponent into betting heavily on second-best cards.

Lawyers use a similar tactic, sometimes called misdirection, that can lure a witness into making damaging commitments. Imagine the deposition of the defendant doctor in a medical malpractice case involving a missed diagnosis. Like most physicians, she would naturally be proud of her professional achievements and eager to talk about them, though her lawyer would no doubt have cautioned her to avoid bragging and to keep her answers short and to the point. More significantly, a claim of expertise on her part could subject her to a higher standard of care. The cross-examiner, therefore, would want to draw her out, hoping to get her to magnify her credentials. Straightforward questioning most likely would not work:

QUESTION: Doctor, do you keep up to date in the medical literature?
ANSWER: Yes.

Well prepared by her counsel, the doctor will surely give a simple answer, revealing minimal information. Misdirection, however, could prompt her to be more expansive:

Q: Doctor, your busy practice must prevent you
　　from keeping completely up to date in the medi-
　　cal literature, isn't that right?
A: Absolutely not, I am totally up to date.
Q: Really? How do you do that?

Now the doctor will be likely to let him have it with both barrels, testifying at length to her devotion to professional journals and her frequent attendance at conferences. She might even claim to have made a special study of the medical condition in question.

Q: Before you saw him, you really didn't know much
　　about my patient's condition, did you?

Thinking that the lawyer wants to minimize her knowledge, she just might be lured into exaggerating it. This technique—reverse bluffing, à la Jack Straus—requires some patient preparation. It won't work with every witness, but it will pay off nicely when it does.

LESSON 6: *Semi-Bluffing*

David Sklansky originated the term *semi-bluff* to describe betting "with a hand which, if called, does not figure to be the best hand at the moment but has a reasonable chance of outdrawing those hands that initially called it." As he elaborates:

When you bet as a semi-bluff, you are rooting to win right there just as you are when you make a pure bluff. However, in contrast to a pure bluff, you still retain a chance of outdrawing your opponent if you are called. . . . Essentially, you are representing a bigger hand than you actually have; however, in contrast to a pure bluff, your hand must have some chance of improving to the best hand.

A semi-bluff may be as simple as betting on a post-flop four flush with two cards to come, or it may involve far more complicated calculations and strategies. In either case, it is essential to count your "outs," meaning the cards that can improve your hand, while simultaneously assessing your opponents' reactions.

Imagine, for example, that you are dealt 8♦ 9♣ and the flop comes 8♠ 10♦ J♥. You could make a semi-bluff raise, representing a completed straight, which would probably drive out any low-to-middling pairs (as well as the rag hands). A high pocket pair might call your bet, but you still have a good chance of winning because you have at least ten outs—any of the four sevens or four queens will complete your straight, and either of the remaining eights will give you three of a kind. In addition, any of the three remaining nines will give you two pair that just might hold up. As with any bluff, this one has its risks. Someone else might have already flopped a straight, or might raise your bet with a set of jacks, at which point you would have to decide whether to reraise (continuing to represent your straight) or fold.

Your chances would be even better, and your incentive to semi-bluff greater, if you had more outs. In the above example, imagine that your hole cards were suited—8♦ 9♦—and the flop was 8♠ 10♦ J♦, giving you both a four flush and an open-ended straight. Now you have 15 good outs (four sevens, four queens, and the additional seven diamonds) and, as before, another 5 mediocre outs (the remaining eights and nines). This hand is virtually made for semi-bluffing because it has so many different ways to win.

Semi-bluffing is well known to trial lawyers. Akin to the poker player's tactic of representing a completed hand, attorneys often propose certain "facts"—sometimes readily available and sometimes not—to recalcitrant witnesses in the hope of either shaking their confidence or shaking out the truth. In the best circumstances, the technique provides three outs. The witness might agree with the lawyer; he might make a tentative and unconvincing denial; or he might brazen it out, only to be impeached later.

Imagine, for example, that the plaintiff in a personal injury case alleges that his back injury has seriously affected his enjoyment of life. One of his most poignant claims is that he can no longer carry his young child in his arms. Doubting the plaintiff's truthfulness, opposing counsel might resort to a time-honored setup and challenge:

Q: Isn't Jennifer Provost your next-door neighbor?
A: Yes, she is.
Q: In fact, your backyards are unfenced and completely open to one another, correct?
A: Yes.
Q: So Jennifer can see right into your yard from her patio, isn't that right?
A: Yes, she can.

Controlling the Opposition

Q: Well, if Jennifer were to testify that she often saw you carrying your kid on your shoulders, would she be lying?

The question is a semi-bluff. The lawyer has represented the availability of impeaching evidence, demanding that the witness either accept it or call his next-door neighbor a liar. This technique must be used sparingly and carefully, if at all, on cross-examination, because ethics principles require a good-faith basis for every question. The approach may be used more broadly, however, in depositions because the rules in most jurisdictions allow discovery of any relevant information, even if inadmissible, so long as it "appears to be reasonably calculated to lead to the discovery of admissible evidence."

One of the most successful semi-bluffs in history occurred in the 1895 London trial of the poet and playwright Oscar Wilde. The Marquess of Queensberry had accused Wilde of engaging in sodomy, and Wilde in turn sued his nemesis for criminal libel. As the first witness, Wilde testified on direct examination that he had never engaged in "gross indecencies" with young men.

On cross-examination, the brilliant barrister Edward Carson had to match wits with one of the most creative minds of that era, or any other. Carson's investigators had located a number of "rent boys" who stated that they had sex with Wilde in exchange for money or gifts. But none of them had yet testified, and it remained to be seen how candid or convincing they would be on the stand or how well they would survive cross-examination. Nonetheless, Carson confronted Wilde with the potential evidence. After repeated prodding about his sex life, Wilde eventually became snappish and careless, just as Carson planned.

CARSON: Were you on familiar terms with Grainger?

WILDE: What do you mean by "familiar terms"?

CARSON: I mean to say did you have him to dine with you or anything of that kind?

WILDE: Never in my life. . . . It is really trying to ask me such a question. No, of course not. He waited on me at table; he did not dine with me.

That was the first opening, and Carson quickly followed up, emphasizing Wilde's earlier claims that he associated freely with working-class youths out of a sense of egalitarianism:

CARSON: I thought he might have sat down. You drew no distinction. . . . You told me yourself—

WILDE: It is a different thing—if it is people's duty to serve, it is their duty to serve; if it is their pleasure to dine, it is their pleasure to dine and their privilege.

Carson continued with the semi-bluff and soon struck gold.

CARSON: Did you ever kiss him?

WILDE: Oh, no, never in my life; he was a peculiarly plain boy.

That was exactly the sort of denial Carson hoped for, though Wilde still had no clue as to how thoroughly he had been baited.

CARSON: He was what?

WILDE: I said I thought him unfortunately—his appearance was so very unfortunately—very ugly— I mean—I pitied him for it.

CARSON: Very ugly?

WILDE: Yes.

CARSON: Do you say that in support of your statement that you never kissed him?

WILDE: No, I don't; it is like asking me if I kissed a
doorpost; it is childish.

CARSON: Didn't you give me as the reason that you
never kissed him that he was too ugly?

WILDE: No.

CARSON: Why did you mention his ugliness?

WILDE: For that reason. If you asked me if I had ever
kissed a doorpost, I should say, "No! Ridiculous!
I shouldn't like to kiss a doorpost." Am I to be
cross-examined on why I shouldn't like to kiss a
doorpost? The questions are grotesque.

Wilde was frantic to dig himself out of the hole, but Carson would not let go of the witness's improvident emphasis
on ugliness.

CARSON: Why did you mention the boy's ugliness?

WILDE: I mentioned it perhaps because you sting
me by an insolent question. . . . You make me
irritable.

CARSON: Did you say the boy was ugly, because I
stung you by an insolent question?

WILDE: Pardon me, you sting me, insult me and try
to unnerve me in every way. At times one says
things flippantly when one should speak more
seriously, I admit that, I admit it—I cannot help
it. That is what you are doing to me.

That was effectively the end of Wilde's case; his own lawyer soon conceded defeat and agreed to a full dismissal (a
criminal prosecution of Wilde would follow, leading to his

ruin). Carson never even had to produce Grainger, or any of
his other witnesses, much less expose them to cross-examination, because the semi-bluff worked.

LESSON 7: *Overplaying*

One of the great ironies of poker is that it is considerably
easier to bluff (or semi-bluff) a good player than a poor one.
Against a poor player, therefore, you will always face the risk
of overplaying your hand. Fancy tactics will tend to backfire because your opponent will be too naive to appreciate or
react to them.

A good player will understand that your bets have meaning, and she will try to out think you. She will realize, for
example, that an initial check followed by a big raise usually means that you have a premium hand (the check was
intended to keep players in the pot, and the subsequent raise
was meant to get more action from the drawing hands). She
will at least consider folding in response, although she might
call your bet if her own hand is decent. Then, once you have
won several showdowns in those situations, you can vary
your play by check-raising as a bluff. Having been trapped
a few times, good players will fold rather than risk another
huge bet.

Other techniques are possible as well, so long as your
opponent is smart enough to react to them. The best bluffs
work because they change the pot odds, making the possible
returns too unattractive to risk calling. Good players recognize this, of course, because they calculate pot odds. For
example, if there is already $1,000 in the pot (with two play-
ers left), a $100 bet would almost always be worth calling

(assuming playable cards) because the pot odds are 11 to 1.
With a $500 bet, however, the pot odds drop to 3 to 1, making
it much more expensive for your opponent to play. Understanding these calculations, a good player will simply do the
math. She will call if she thinks there is a 50% chance you are
bluffing, but she will fold if she thinks that the probability
is 25% or less. An even larger bet—say $1,000 or $2,000—will
shift the calculus even more dramatically, making it nearly
impossible for a sophisticated player to stay in the pot.

Novices and other poor players never calculate the pot
odds, so they seldom realize when they are making bad bets.
They don't even try to interpret your moves, so they are not
susceptible to sophisticated plays. Doyle Brunson says that
"against a low-grade player you simply make the obvious
play." Instead of getting fancy, "you play *fundamentally* better
(rather than strategically better) than a weak player."

Brunson tells the story of an obviously weak player who
entered the 1977 World Championship Tournament. "He
was the supreme example of a *calling station*—a player who's
next-to-impossible to bluff." Brunson quickly realized that
there was no way to outmaneuver a player who was likely to
call every bet. "I quickly decided that if I was in the pot with
him, I was going to show him a hand. And, if he got lucky
enough to beat me . . . well, he was going to beat a hand."

Not every professional, it appears, was so astute, as
Brunson explained in his uniquely emphatic and ellipses-
laden prose:

> There were other very good players in the Tourna-
> ment who tried to *run over* him—tried to force him
> out of a pot. They would bluff at him constantly . . .
> and they were **rarely** successful.

You simply **can't** bluff a **bad** player . . . because
a bad player will play when he's got some kind of a
hand and will pass when he doesn't have a hand.

All you have to know is if he's in the pot . . . he's
got something. And you're not going to get him out
of the pot by trying to bluff him.

Above all . . . **you** *don't* **want to gamble with a**
weak **player**. Forget about that . . . show him a hand.
You do very fundamental things against a bad player.
Obvious things. That is . . . no tricks . . . no strategic
plays . . . nothing fancy. Play straight-forward poker
against a weak player.

Yardley put it a bit more succinctly: "Never bluff a simpleton," he said. Poor players will be so busy looking at their
own cards that they won't try to figure out your hand. Strong
players will fold when they believe you have superior cards,
but once "a sucker stays it is hard to drive him out."

Alan Morrison, the long-time director of the Public Citi-
zen Litigation Group, tells the following story about opposing lawyers who seriously overplayed their hand.

In the late 1980s, Merrill Williams was a temporary paralegal working for Wyatt Tarrent & Combs, defense counsel for Brown & Williamson in tobacco liability litigation.
In the course of his work, Williams read many documents
that revealed unpleasant secrets about the tobacco industry.
Himself a long-time smoker, he began secretly to remove and
copy hundreds of documents from the Brown & Williamson
file (without much difficulty and without being detected,
although he did this over the course of many weeks).

Williams was laid off in 1992 and shortly afterward suffered a heart attack, which he attributed in part to his ciga-

rette habit. He consulted an attorney about a possible suit against B&W, informing the lawyer about the purloined documents. The lawyer, in turn, wrote to B&W with a demand for money damages, revealing Williams's identity and the existence of the copied documents.

Brown & Williamson responded aggressively, quickly obtaining a temporary restraining order (which later became a preliminary injunction), forbidding Williams from discussing the documents with anyone, including his own lawyers.

At that point, Morrison became involved in the case. He moved to modify the injunction, on the ground that it could not have been intended to prevent Williams from speaking with his own attorneys. Brown & Williamson resisted, however, and the court denied the motion. When the appellate court refused to intervene, Williams was barred from obtaining effective legal advice.

It seemed at first like a stunning victory for the tobacco company's lawyers, but it turned out that they had overplayed their hand. Here is how Morrison describes the events that followed:

> So our client couldn't talk to us. This meant that we refused to produce him for deposition since we could not prepare him. But even worse, it meant he could not ask us for advice, and he therefore did not tell us that he had even more copied documents than originally disclosed. But he did talk with other lawyers, including the Mississippi Attorney General, who was preparing a massive suit against the tobacco industry.
>
> The Mississippi A.G. persuaded Merrill that it was permissible to give him copies of the documents,

since he was in law enforcement. I would have coun-
termanded that advice if I had been allowed to talk
with my client. But the preliminary injunction prevented that, and Merrill never realized that he was
violating the injunction.

That same enforced ignorance led him to believe
that it was allowable to send the documents to Con-
gressman Henry Waxman and to the Food and Drug
Administration, who made them public.

Pressing their advantage, the B&W lawyers thought they
could intimidate Merrill Williams into cooperating with
them. They got what they wanted—or what they thought they
wanted—from the preliminary injunction, but of course it
boomeranged. Williams was far from a simpleton, but he did
not understand the full extent of the injunction. Deprived
of advice from his own lawyers, he naively assumed that he
could give the materials to government officials.

That was a devastating result for B&W. Public exposure
made its situation infinitely worse and eventually led to
one of the largest civil lawsuits in U.S. history. Assuming
that they could bludgeon a poor paralegal into compliance,
the tobacco lawyers badly outsmarted themselves. Merrill
Williams, it turns out, did not know enough to be afraid
of them.

LESSON 8: *Calling Bluffs*

One of the most potentially expensive moments in poker
occurs when you announce, "I'm calling your bluff," and
throw one last stack of chips into the pot in the hope that

you have correctly read your opponent's hand. If you are correct—that he was representing strength while holding losers—you stand to win a lot of money. But if you are wrong—the big bets were backed up by big cards—you have just wasted your money. There is obviously a great art in responding to bluffs and possible bluffs, and there are no simple answers.

The first, and probably the best, defense to bluffing is to play solid fundamental poker. Faced with a large opening bet, you should often just fold your hand unless you are holding pretty strong cards. Although it sometimes pays to play a drawing hand, a large bet generally makes it too expensive to see the next card. There is no shame in folding in these circumstances, whether your opponent is bluffing or not, because the expected value of your hand is too small in relation to the bet.

With a premium or playable hand, the calculus is trickier. Your first defense is observational. Against a poor or mediocre player, you can often pick up a sign, or tell, that lets you know whether he is bluffing. I will talk more about tells in the "Spades" section ("Digging for Information"), but for now it is sufficient to note that your opponents' tells usually reveal themselves over time, as you match their behavior to the patterns in their play. It is difficult, though not impossible, to accurately interpret the quirks and mannerisms of a new player who, if he is any good, is trying to deceive you.

In any event, if you are convinced that a player is bluffing, you can always find out by calling his last bet. He will have to show you his cards, and you will have your answer. This can provide a cheap lesson if you do it early in the game, preferably in a small pot. There is always the possibility, however, that you are facing a genius who allowed himself to be caught early in order to exploit the nuts in a later hand. Then again, if you think you are facing someone of that caliber, well, you probably ought to find another table (unless you have comparable skills yourself).

Above all, you do not want to become a "calling station," someone who invariably calls opponents' bets in order to "keep them honest." Yes, you will avoid being bluffed, but at the cost of losing hand after hand to better cards. It bears remembering that the point of poker is to avoid losing under any circumstances, not simply to avoid being bluffed. Ultimately, you want to vary your defensive play in more or less the same way that you vary your other bets. Sometimes you call bluffs, and sometimes you fold, with no discernible pattern. That may encourage your opponents to overbluff, which will in turn allow you to beat them with solid cards.

David Sklansky adds two further refinements for either stopping or inducing bluffs. You can limit your opponents' bluffing by representing strength in the opening rounds. Your early bet will show that you intend to back your cards, which will discourage anyone else from bluffing heavily on rags. Conversely, an early check may induce later players to attempt to steal the pot by bluffing (especially if you have already folded a couple of small hands in like circumstances). You could then either call or reraise when the bet comes back to you, having gotten your opponent to contribute some extra money to the pot.

One more thought: There will be times when the pot odds dictate calling the last bet, even if you are pretty sure it is not a bluff. Let's say that you are dealt K♥ K♠ in Texas Hold'em, and the flop comes 6♣ 7♣ 10♦. Your opponent bets strongly, representing either a straight or a flush draw, and you call. The K♦ falls on the turn, leading to more heavy betting and a decent-sized pot. Finally, 8♣ shows up on the

Controlling the Opposition

river. This is obviously bad news, as your opponent might well have either a straight (with a nine in the hole) or a flush (with any 2 of the 10 remaining clubs). Nonetheless, it may make sense to call his bet. Your three kings are the nut set, so you are giving away the entire pot if you fold your winners. On the other hand, you are only risking a single bet if you call (and your opponent made his straight or flush).

There are lawyers who bluff even more than card players. In fact, they go beyond bluffing: They bluster, rage, threaten, and storm over issues great and small. Sometimes it makes sense simply to fold. Why argue over trivialities like the wording of an interrogatory answer? Sure, she is probably bluffing about filing a motion to compel, but it is still easier to rewrite the answer than to argue a motion. Sometimes, however, you simply have to call the bluff—turning down a lowball offer even as counsel insists that her client "hasn't authorized a penny more"—based on your reading of the situation and the available alternatives.

And sometimes you will want to induce bluffing, confident that it will backfire for your opponent. Some lawyers, for example, tend to be overbearing in depositions. Such an attorney often assumes a swaggering demeanor, as though he can intimidate a witness into being more forthcoming. Of course, it is a bluff. Deponents have to answer truthfully and fully, but they do not have to answer expansively or at great length. As we will see in the next lesson, there are efficient techniques for getting deponents to amplify their answers, but blustering is not one of them. Threats are usually counterproductive; the more the lawyer bludgeons, the less the witness talks. Defending counsel, therefore, might actually want to encourage a display of extravagant arrogance from the opposition, realizing that it will probably keep the wit-

ness from volunteering answers.

LESSON 9: *Loose Wiring*

Mike Caro, who styles himself the "mad genius of poker," believes that you can best influence your opponents by understanding his Law of Loose Wiring. In brief, Caro postulates that many players' decisions are ultimately snap judgments, determined as frequently by whim as by cunning. Even the most seasoned professionals, he says, "can be impressionable, irritable, playful, [or] capricious." Depending upon their mood and the specific situation in the game, your opponents' reactions can range from brilliant to silly, and back again, almost without notice. The reason for this, Caro explains, is that most poker decisions are spontaneous, rather than the result of careful planning. Moreover, there are "relatively few overwhelmingly strong or weak hands that dictate an exact tactic." Thus, card players are constantly making "borderline decisions" about whether to raise, call, or fold, and borderline decisions are highly sensitive to outside influences.

All of this leads to Caro's Law of Loose Wiring, which predicts that players' actions are not fully predictable:

> If choices *are not* clearly connected to their benefits, people usually interact in ways that make outcomes unpredictable. If choices *are* clearly connected to their benefits, people sometimes react in ways that make outcomes unpredictable.

In other words, your opponents themselves often do not know precisely how they will react until the very last moment and sometimes not until their decisions have already been made. Unlike a chess match, in which skillful players plot four and five successive moves at a time, poker players tend to make many of their choices impulsively, if not by whim.

Uncertainty is always discomforting, and never more so than under pressure and when money is at stake. Thus, whenever their decisions can go either way—which is most of the time—your opponents will be "looking for anything to direct their borderline decisions." It is your job, and your opportunity, to provide the right impetus, making their whims work for you.

Caro's rule could just as easily be called "loose tethering," meaning that most players are only loosely tied to their own strategies. But "loose wiring" implies a certain vulnerable instability, more in keeping with Caro's chosen persona as a mad genius.

Either way, it is probably true that more lawyers are tightly wound than loosely wired, and it is probably a poor idea to believe that you can take advantage of opposing counsel's presumed snap decisions.

But witnesses are another story. Many witnesses, perhaps most, perfectly fit Caro's definition of loose wiring. They may have a broad idea of how they want to respond in general, but they have almost no control over their reactions in borderline situations.

Consider the deposition of an opposing party. No doubt she has been well prepared by her own counsel, instructed repeatedly to keep her answers short and to avoid volunteering. A capable opposing lawyer will have taken her through a practice deposition (or many practice depositions, depend-

ing on the size of the case), trying to show her how easy it is
to forget instructions and begin rambling. The classic example involves a simple request:

Q: Do you happen to have the time?
A: Sure, it's almost 2:30.

That is the wrong answer, of course, because it went
beyond the actual question. In a deposition, if nowhere else
in human interactions, the correct answer is simply "yes."
If the lawyer wants more information, he will have to ask
another question. In the world of litigation, that makes perfect sense.

But no matter how much she is prepared, sandpapered,
woodshedded, cautioned, or admonished, a typical deponent will never be more than tenuously committed to the
proposition that monosyllabic answers are best. Instead,
the natural tendency to amplify and explain will always be
lurking in the background. In clear-cut situations, she will
probably be able to hold the line, but in more ambiguous
circumstances—on Caro's loose-wiring borderline—she will
be looking for cues to help her decide whether the answer
should be curt or expansive.

You can usually get a deponent to start talking by asking open-ended questions, using the standard newspaper
reporter's inquiries: what, where, when, why, and how? A
disciplined witness, however, might well be able to stick to
short, uninformative answers.

Q: How were you hurt?
A: In an automobile accident.
Q: What happened next?
A: I went to the hospital.

Q: Why are you suing?

A: Because I am disabled.

Q: How are you disabled?

A: I cannot work.

In all but the most unnaturally tight-lipped cases, how-ever, there will be longer answers straining to be released. All the witness needs is a reason or an excuse to push her over the edge. If you are able to provide one—*kaboom!*—the law of loose wiring will take over. Sometimes the nudge can be as modest as a pregnant pause, using eye contact or a friendly gesture to signal the witness to continue. Just as nature abhors a vacuum, most deponents are uncomfortable with silence; they will often begin speaking to fill the space.

Q: How were you hurt?

A: In an automobile accident.

Q: And . . .

With hand extended and a gentle nod of the head, counsel can probably entice the witness to provide additional details. But if that does not work, another query or two might do the trick.

Q: Why do you think that the accident was the other driver's fault?

Q: Please explain why you could not avoid the acci-dent.

Q: What would you like to say to the defendant about what he did to you?

Just remember Caro's law. The witness is looking for any-thing that will help her decide how to answer the questions. Her lawyers have exhorted her to be terse, so blunt question-

ing will only tend to make her stick with their advice. An
invitation or, better yet, a good reason could have the opposite result. With the proper incentives, most witnesses can
be shaken loose from their moorings, untethered from their
lawyers' instructions, and with a little luck, rewired.

LESSON 10: *Folding Winners*

You also need to be alert to your own potential for loose
wiring, the tendency to make an irrevocable decision on the
basis of your initial impression or belief. Amarillo Slim Preston once said, "If you can't fold the winning hand, you can't
play poker." He did not mean it literally, of course. If you
know that you have the winning hand, you will surely play
until the end. But if you only *think* that you have the winning
hand, well, then you have to be open to the possibility that
you are wrong. And once that thought arises, you must be
willing to fold your hand no matter how good it looks and
no matter how large the pot. Remember, the biggest losers
are second-best hands.

Using a story about Doyle Brunson, Alvarez describes
the "art of folding at the highest level." In an insanely high-
stakes game in Las Vegas, Brunson found himself holding
pocket aces, the best possible cards. He bet strongly but was
called by two other players. The flop was even more favorable
to Brunson—A 2 4, unsuited—and he moved in with $25,000.
Surprisingly, both other players called. The turn brought
another deuce, giving Brunson aces full of deuces, a seemingly unbeatable full house. Curious about the other players'
intentions, Brunson checked. Surprisingly, the next player
made a large bet. Even more surprisingly, the other player

moved all in, raising the bet to $100,000. After a long hesitation, Brunson folded his full house.

The dealer dealt another four on the river, making the board A 2 4 2 4. The two remaining players showed their hands, and each had four of a kind. One had quad deuces, and the other won with quad fours. Brunson made the right play, but how did he know to fold his powerful hand? Alvarez provides this explanation:

> When Brunson bet big before the flop, [the other players] would have read him for a high pair in the hole. . . . So they would have had to have pairs in their hands to call him. And when he bet again strongly after the flop, what else could either of them have called him with except trips? So when the board paired, Brunson knew one of them must have made quads. Even so, it took exceptionally iron discipline and cold-eyed calculation to fold his massive hand.

Brunson lost more than $30,000 on that hand, but he saved himself a further $100,000 by folding. The ultimate winner got lucky when he drew the last four, but he actually misplayed the hand by betting with his trip fours against Brunson's full house and the other player's quad deuces. In the long run, he will lose a lot of money if he continues to bet that way, with just one out on the river. Just ask Amarillo Slim.

The same rule applies to lawyers, though not always on quite so grand a scale. At the simplest level, you must be willing to abandon a line of questioning—no matter how powerful it once seemed—as soon as you realize that it may be counterproductive. You might have some dynamite impeaching evidence on a witness, say a prior felony conviction or an embarrassing personal indiscretion, that you cannot wait to use on cross-examination. But if the witness turns out to be especially dignified and respectable during direct examination, clearly earning the jury's sympathy, you will need to consider "folding" that particular winner lest you alienate the jurors by appearing inappropriately disrespectful or unnecessarily rude.

Sometimes, the stakes are dramatically higher. In 1999, an African immigrant named Amadou Diallo was standing on the front stoop of his Bronx apartment building. Something about him drew the attention of four New York City police officers on patrol as part of the department's Street Crimes Unit. They called out to Diallo, who reached for his wallet, presumably intending to produce his identification. In a tragedy that shook the nation, the police reacted to Diallo's movement by drawing their guns and firing 41 shots at the unarmed man. A total of 15 bullets struck Diallo, killing him on the spot.

The police officers claimed afterward that they had mistaken Diallo's wallet for a gun. But New York City was outraged, and the Bronx district attorney indicted the police officers for murder. Following a change of venue, the case came to trial in Albany the next year. After the prosecution case, which relied heavily on the needless barrage of 41 shots, each of the four police officers testified for the defense. Some of them wept on the stand. They all apologized repeatedly. One officer testified that he held the dying Diallo in his arms immediately after the shooting, attempting to resuscitate him while begging "please don't die." They explained their mistaken reactions, but did not attempt to justify the killing. In other words, they portrayed themselves as sorrowful actors in a terrible tragedy, but not as murderers.

The prosecution response was to dwell heavily on the 41 shots, arguing that there was no explanation for the killing other than murder. The jury thought otherwise, however, ignoring even the lesser included offenses and acquitting all of the defendants on all counts.

Looking back at the trial, the prosecutors must surely have believed at the outset that they had a winning case. A wallet looks nothing like a gun, and the fusillade of 41 bullets seemed to show a relentlessness out of all proportion to the police officers' actual situation. But murder requires proof of malice or premeditation. Absent direct evidence, it was obviously going to be nearly impossible to get the jury to infer that the remorseful police officers had gunned down Diallo with murder in their hearts. Nonetheless, the prosecution stuck with the murder theory, arguing it to the very end. Many observers believe that the murder charge was so rhetorically overpowering that it virtually blotted out even the possibility of conviction of a lesser included offense, such as manslaughter, making the resulting acquittals inevitable.

In retrospect, the prosecutors in the Diallo case might have been successful if they had been willing to fold their murder case, no matter how powerful it seemed, in favor of a manslaughter charge. As it was, they lost everything.

LESSON 11: *Establishing Patterns*

There is a saying among some public defenders that their job is to "win bench trials and lose jury trials." No lawyers ever intend to lose, of course, but public defenders are in an unusual situation in that they have little or no control over their caseloads. And let's face it, most of their clients are clearly guilty, and many of their cases are basically hopeless. Nonetheless, it is a public defender's honorable obligation to present the best possible defense for clients who wish to proceed to trial and to obtain the best possible dispositions for clients who want to plead guilty.

Putting plea bargains to one side for the moment, we can now look at the public defenders' decision matrix (or more precisely, their recommendation-to-clients matrix) when it comes to opting for bench or jury trials. In the best cases, where there is a good chance of demonstrating reasonable doubt, it makes sense to take bench trials, simply because judges are more predictable than jurors. If the defense lawyer sees a glaring weakness or gap in the prosecution case, then it is likely that the judge will see it too. A jury trial is always a gamble, even for a powerful case, so the best option is to present the most winnable cases to the judge alone.

In the least winnable cases, however, the public defenders' calculation is precisely the opposite. If the defense lawyer believes that the prosecution case is overwhelming, it is almost certain that the judge will see it that way as well, meaning that a bench trial would be nearly hopeless—a "slow plea of guilty," as another saying goes. In this situation, a jury's unpredictability becomes a benefit to the defendant, especially since it only takes one not-guilty vote to produce a hung jury. And beyond that, anything might happen, including a lightning strike or an outright acquittal. Consequently, a savvy public defender will always attempt to present her strongest cases to the court (thus, winning bench trials) and her weakest cases to juries (thus, losing jury trials).

And that brings us to plea bargains. A lawyer who astutely divides her cases between bench and jury trials should also have two advantages in plea bargaining. First, she will establish that she can tell which cases are potential winners, which will give her greater credibility when she tells the prosecution that a particular case is strong. In addition, she will show that she is a dangerous adversary, willing to take weak cases to trial rather than settle for a bad bargain. And if she wins even a fraction of those trials, she will give the prosecutors a further incentive to make good offers to her clients.

Poker players will recognize this dynamic immediately. Our hypothetical public defender is demonstrating a pattern—playing strong hands strongly at bench trials—and then varying it in unpredictable ways. The jury trials are roughly the equivalent of bluffs, but the occasional acquittals mean that she sometimes turns out to be holding winners. More important, plea bargaining is also a form of bluffing, backed by the public defender's implicit threat of taking the case to trial in the absence of a decent offer.

In other words, the public defender can exert maximum influence over the prosecutor by establishing a pattern that both changes the effective odds and makes outcomes unpredictable. As a result, the prosecutors are kept constantly off balance during the negotiations. They know that the public defender is adept at evaluating her cases, but they never know whether any given case is truly strong from the defense perspective, or whether the public defender is representing better cards than she really holds. And even if they believe that they have a strong case, there is always the possibility of a "wild card" jury verdict. Thus, thanks to the public defender's long-term tactics, the prosecutors have the maximum incentive to make attractive offers when plea bargaining.

The value of setting a pattern can be enormous, because your opponent can never know when, or how, you will diverge from it. In the 1972 World Series of Poker, Amarillo

Slim faced Puggy Pearson head to head at the final table. Slim played a loose game, raising blind on hand after hand and successfully stealing pots from the more conservative Pearson. Then Slim made a staggering bet of $51,000 on what turned out to be the last hand. Pearson called the bet, convinced that Slim was bluffing again. But this time, Slim held the nuts and won the world championship.

Card players are free to create patterns of behavior—or at least to try—however they choose. They can overplay some hands or intentionally lose others, planning to set up their opponents and recoup heavily in the future. Lawyers' conduct, of course, is far more constrained. Ethics principles prohibit a lawyer from sacrificing one client for the benefit of another. You may not fold a good case or overplay a bad one for the purpose of extracting better settlements in the future. Consistent with client approval, however, you may adopt an optimal strategy for handling cases while reaping collateral benefits for the clients who follow.

LESSON 12: *Implication and Storytelling*

As we have seen, the optimum betting strategy in poker—and the best way to influence your opponents' play—can be boiled down to two general principles:

Rule One: Show weakness when your hand is strong and strength when your hand is weak.

Rule Two: Occasionally violate Rule One in unpredictable ways.

The point, of course, is to keep your opponents guessing about the true value of your hand and to make them guess incorrectly as frequently as possible. This strategy is most effective when you succeed in *implying* a particular hand, meaning that you cause your opponents to think that they know what you are holding. Unpredictability, therefore, does not mean betting wildly or out of the blue. That will simply convince your opponents that they don't know what you are doing, making them cautious when you want them to be decisive (and decisively wrong). Instead, you should use your cards and bets to tell a story, the more specific the better.

Imagine, for example, that you are dealt two unsuited low cards in Texas Hold'em, but you decide that the table is bluffable. A strong opening bet will represent a high pocket pair, probably aces or kings. If an ace or king falls on the flop, another strong bet will be necessary to imply a set. But if a low pair flops, your bet will probably imply two pair, meaning that you will not be able to bluff anyone who flopped trips of their own. Given your "story," that situation would be dangerous indeed against decent opposition.

Now, assume the same initial situation—low cards in the hole and an intention to bluff if you can. This time, however, you check (or perhaps call someone else's small bet), indicating a drawing hand. If the flop then shows two suited cards, let's say a couple of small clubs, a moderate bet would imply a four flush. If another club falls on the turn, a large bet would signal that you had filled your hand; anything less would reveal your bluff. Conversely, a nonclub on fourth street would ordinarily call for at most a modest bet (unless it paired another card on the board), because anything else would be inconsistent with your implied club flush.

Bobby Baldwin used a similar strategy in the 1978 World Series of Poker when he faced Crandall Addington at the final table. Addington called Baldwin's small pre-flop bet, and the flop came Q♦ 4♦ 3♣. Baldwin immediately bet $30,000, representing a flush or a straight draw. Addington, who now had a pair of queens, called without hesitation. The turn brought the A♦. Baldwin moved in with $95,000, strongly implying a completed flush.[2] Addington thought it over for a while and then folded. Baldwin's flush play was just too convincing to risk such a huge bet. Baldwin wasn't finished storytelling, however. He made a point of showing his hole cards, the 9♥ 10♥, revealing his bluff. Now Addington would have to doubt his own instincts, shaking his play until he was soon eliminated.

The same technique can also be used in reverse, as Johnny Chan demonstrated against Erik Seidel in the final hand at the 1988 WSOP. Neither player bet in the initial round, and the flop brought Q♠ 10♦ 8♦. Chan checked and Seidel, who now had a pair of queens, bet $50,000. The turn was a rag, and both players checked. Another rag fell on fifth street, and Chan checked again. Convinced now that Chan was holding weak cards, Seidel bet all of his chips on his own relatively weak pair of queens. That massive bet should have caused Chan to fold even two pair, which seemed like the best hand he could possibly have. Instead, Chan called the bet and turned over his hole cards, the J♣ 9♣. He had

---

[2] A straight was also possible, but much less likely. There were ten remaining diamonds that could complete Baldwin's flush, but only eight cards—deuces and fives—that could fill the inside straight. Furthermore, it was almost unimaginable, and therefore unbelievable, that Baldwin would have opened the pre-flop betting with only a deuce and a five in the hole, as opposed to a couple of fairly high diamonds.

flopped a straight but concealed it in order to draw Seidel more deeply into the pot. Seidel never would have risked his entire stack if Chan had been betting heavily, but Chan's two rounds of checking had successfully implied a much weaker hand—winning him the world championship.

Unlike card players, lawyers are not free simply to imply anything they want. Trials must be based on truth, not intentional misrepresentations. Nonetheless, there is a lesson to be learned from the art of implication. A cohesive story is far more convincing than a random assemblage of facts. A card player is most successful when he begins with a single narrative, if you will, and supports it as the hand proceeds: "I am drawing to a flush," or "I don't have much in my hand." If the narrative is reasonable and consistent, his opponents will interpret new information—the following cards—in a way that is consistent with the overall story.

Trials work in nearly the same way (though it is crucial to remember that the stories must be true). A successful trial theory will not depend merely on the accumulation of facts. Rather, it will begin with a story that makes sense of the facts that follow. Here is an example of that phenomenon at work.

On December 22, 1984, a reclusive technician named Bernhard Goetz entered a subway car in New York City. He was soon confronted by four young African-American men, who either asked for or demanded money. Instead of complying, Goetz pulled an illegal revolver from his pocket and shot each of the four, gravely wounding each of them. Goetz quickly fled the train, but he later turned himself in to the police in New Hampshire, where he gave a lengthy videotaped statement.

The story of the "subway gunman" made headlines around the world. To some, Goetz was a dangerous racist, who took random vengeance on four innocent (or nearly innocent) teenagers, while recklessly endangering everyone else in the subway car. To others, he was a heroic vigilante, standing up to predators at a time when the New York City police seemed helpless in the face of a mounting crime wave.

Goetz was indicted on charges of attempted murder, assault, reckless endangerment, and criminal possession of a firearm. Brought to trial in a Manhattan courtroom, he predictably pled self-defense, claiming that he reasonably believed that he was the victim of a forcible robbery. At the time, mugging was an incessant problem on the New York City transit system, so Goetz's claim was likely to resonate with a jury of Manhattanites.

But there was—literally—a huge gap in his story. After he had already shot all four of the young men, Goetz saw one of them, Darrell Cabey, lying on the subway floor. Walking over to him, Goetz said, "You look okay, here's another," and fired one more round, severing Cabey's spine and rendering him a paraplegic. This act, the prosecutor argued, could not possibly have come in self-defense. There was too much time—in fact, there was a pause—between the alleged robbery and the final shot. So even if the confrontation began with Goetz as a victim, it ended with him in the self-assigned role of a cold-blooded hit man.

Defense witnesses, however, testified that there had been no pause in the shooting, but rather that he fired five times in quick succession. Therein lay the difference between innocence and guilt. If all five shots had been in response to an attempted robbery, then the claim of self-defense was plausible, and Goetz might be acquitted. If there had been a gap in the firing, however, then the shooting of Cabey was, in legal terms, a separate transaction for which Goetz had no defense.

Recognizing that the time gap, or lack of one, was crucial to its case, the prosecution took a cumulative approach, attempting to use the interruption in the shooting to establish the theory that Goetz was the aggressor. The matter probably seemed incontrovertible, since Goetz had admitted the pause when he gave his videotaped statement to the New Hampshire police.

In contrast, the defense began with its story and worked backward toward the facts. In the defense narrative, Bernhard Goetz was purely a victim, terrorized by thugs in New York. The four young men on the train were, in fact, violent predators, all of whom had criminal records. One of the four, James Ramseur, had been convicted of the rape and sodomy of a pregnant woman. All of them had menaced Goetz, surrounding him as they demanded money. The looming threat caused the meek technician to panic, firing all five shots on automatic pilot.

While the prosecution theory was based on a single, precise factual question, defense counsel made the alleged pause a much smaller part of a much larger story. In the big picture, Goetz's fearful reactions were made to seem reasonable—in which case, the conclusion followed that he fired all five shots without interruption.

The jury dismissed Goetz's confession—that he deliberately stood over Cabey and shot him a second time—as the product of stress and confusion. The inconvenient fact did not fit the broader theory, so the jury simply disregarded it. Stories win every time.

The novelist James McManus is the most successful poker journalist ever to play the game. As he chronicles in his memoir, *Positively Fifth Street*, he was assigned by *Harper's Magazine* to cover the 2000 World Series of Poker. Instead, he used his entire advance to enter the competition and eventually finished in fifth place, winning nearly $250,000. A decent amateur player, he concedes that there was a good deal of luck involved in his triumph. But he dispenses a good deal of practical wisdom as well.

One of McManus's key observations is about the value of patience. "Lying in wait is what good poker players do best," he says. "More than any other character flaw, overeagerness is what does in the rest of us. As your stack dwindles and the antes and blinds keep doubling, you become less and less capable of waiting for sensible hole cards."

There are actually two advantages to patient play. First, you will increase the quality of your own hand selection if you are willing to wait for the right cards. And perhaps equally valuable, you will give your opponents time to make mistakes. If you play few enough hands, it is almost certain that someone else will be playing too many.

No less an authority than Herbert Yardley extolled the virtue of his own forbearance, folding hand after hand while earning the nickname "Old Adhesive." Then, when he finally entered a pot—often bluffing when it was his turn to deal—the other players would fold precipitously, lacking the patience to see his cards. And when he did have a winning hand, he would quietly wait for other players to begin the raising, drawing their foolish money into the pot. Let the suckers "do your betting for you," he advised, "because they are usually wild players who bet on everything and anything" while you preserve the option "to stay, raise, or fold your hand."

Let the suckers bet for you. That might be the best advice of all for both card players and lawyers. Toki Clark, a solo practitioner in Columbus, Ohio, tells a terrific story in which patience conquers all.

Her client, the owner of a tattoo parlor, was charged under the Ohio RICO statute with stealing more than $500,000 from a railroad yard over a three-year period. After one mistrial and one hung jury, her client was looking at the third expensive trial and facing nearly 60 years in prison. "There I was," says Clark:

> Black and female, representing a White client who did not have two nickels to rub together. . . . We surely looked like a rag-tag team compared to the smooth prosecutors and suave police detective across the aisle, who wanted my client bad. Five witnesses got on the stand and testified that my client was right there with them when they committed major thefts from the rail yards. Even his female first cousin testified against him. Despite this, my instinct told me that the jurors were pulling for us. I knew it. I could just feel it.

Then, toward the end of the trial, Clark asked the prosecutor to hand her a document. He replied crudely, though under his breath, referring to Clark with a four-letter vulgarity for the female anatomy. Clark's client heard the slur and understandably insisted that she complain to the judge. "He wanted me to rant and rave about the name that the prosecutor called me," she says. After giving it some quick thought, Clark realized that patience would be more effec-

tive than outrage. "Never interrupt your opponent while he
is busy destroying himself," she explained.

I told my client that I knew we had the jurors in our boat, and if the prosecutor viewed me in that term, then that sentiment would come across in how he treated me for the remainder of the trial. And the prosecutor did just that. He got out of control and alienated the jury. It was extremely rewarding when they came back with a Not Guilty verdict.

Toki Clark's winning strategy calls to mind another of McManus's keen insights: "Like jujitsu and asymmetrical warfare, poker is about transferring leverage and wiping out bad guys efficiently." Just so.

Knowledge is power in almost every setting where power makes a difference, but seldom more than in poker and law. In both pursuits, there is a premium on reliable information, as adversaries are constantly trying to spot each other's weaknesses and outwit their opponents.

In the film *Legally Blonde*, Reese Witherspoon plays a California sorority girl named Elle Woods who is trying to reinvent herself as a Harvard law student. She turns out to be smarter than anyone suspected and is asked to assist one of her professors in defending a young woman charged with murdering her very wealthy 60-year-old husband. As proof of motive, the prosecution calls the couple's hunky pool boy, who testifies that he was having an affair with the attractive defendant. He seems to be lying, but how to prove it?

During a recess, Elle finds herself standing in line for the water fountain, as the prosecution witness takes his sweet time drinking. Frustrated by his rudeness, she taps her foot impatiently. "Don't stamp your little last-season Prada shoes at me, honey," he sneers. Fuming at the insult (she wouldn't be caught dead in last season's shoes), it takes a moment for Elle to realize the significance of the encounter. A straight man would never recognize designer shoes, much less identify them by season. The pool boy must be gay; therefore, he couldn't have been having an affair with her client! Racing to the courtroom, she shares her discovery with a young lawyer on the defense team. He shrewdly cross-examines the witness, exposing him as a liar. Things are looking better for the defendant.

Later, however, the victim's daughter provides damning evidence against the defendant. "I saw her kneeling over my father, covered in his blood," she says. By this time, Elle has taken over the entire defense, including the cross-examination.

Q: Why couldn't anyone find the gun?
A: Because your client had time to stash it.
Q: Well, why didn't you hear the shot?
A: Because I was in the shower, washing my hair.

Another light goes on, as Elle realizes that this witness is lying too. "Didn't you say that you had a perm that day? Isn't it the first rule of permanent waves that you can't get your hair wet for at least 24 hours? And don't you know that because you've been getting perms all your life?"

Flummoxed, the witness confesses that she did the shooting herself, blaming the crime on her stepmother out of petulant anger. All charges are dismissed. Admiring reporters gather around Elle, asking how she cracked the case.

"The rules of hair care are simple and finite," Elle replies. "Any Cosmo girl would have known."

The *Legally Blonde* story is fanciful, of course, but the lesson is valid. Sometimes a case can turn on the slightest insight or smallest fact. In the post-Enron prosecution of Arthur Andersen & Co., for example, the jury ended up basing its guilty verdict on the content of a single e-mail, out of thousands of documents that were introduced in evidence. It takes an exhaustive accumulation of information and thoughtful—perhaps even cunning—analysis to put together a winning case, or hand.

LESSON 1: *Knowledge Is Power*

In both poker and law, the types of information fall into three rough categories. The "up" cards in poker are always public knowledge, equally available to everyone, never to be hidden or changed. In that regard, they correspond to documents produced on discovery and to deposition testimony. Once disclosed, this information is no longer private. It can be used by anyone to seek out more information, to influence negotiation, or (consistent with the rules of evidence) for introduction at trial. The "hole" cards, in contrast, are secret and proprietary. Each player controls access to her own pocket cards, exposing them, if at all, only if her final bet has been called. The legal analogue is confidential information, which a party never needs to reveal unless she herself "opens the door," that being the litigation equivalent of raising a bet. Finally, there is the broad middle ground of information—the bets, calls, feints, and ploys that are neither fully disclosed (because they are often disguised and must be interpreted) nor fully privileged (because they occur in plain view).

Skillful players, and lawyers, must master all three categories of information. You must know how to exploit the up cards, whether (and how) to reveal your hole cards, and, most intriguingly, how to read your opponents' signals, whether intentional or unintentional, while camouflaging your own.

In poker, this is done by betting—throwing chips of varying value into the pot while gauging the reactions of everyone else at the table. According to Alvarez:

> Chips are not just a way of keeping score; they combine with the cards to form the very language of the game. What you do with your chips—how and when you bet or check or raise—is a way of communicating with your opponents. . . . The questions you ask and the answers you receive may be misleading—a gigantic bet may be a sign of weakness, an attempt to drive the other players out of the pot because you do not have the hand you purport to have—but the combination of cards and money and position at the table creates a complex pattern of information (or illusion) that controls the flow of the game.

Instead of chips, lawyers use questions, requests, demands, arguments, claims, and motions when attempting to outmaneuver their opponents. With each side doing its best to intertwine candid, ambiguous, and illusory information, the winner is usually the lawyer who is best able to untangle the knotty facts. This is never more true than in negotiation, where "puffery" is explicitly permitted by the *Model Rules of Professional Conduct*, and no good lawyer would ever willingly reveal his true bottom line.

Whether they are openly negotiating or just exploring the possibility, opposing attorneys often expend considerable time and energy attempting to maneuver each other into making the first offer. Neither one wants to make the opening move, for fear that it will be interpreted as a sign of weakness. Even worse, each lawyer inevitably worries that she has miscalculated the value of her case and may end up giving away the store if she cannot get the other side's offer first. Indeed, "never make the first offer" has practically become a mantra in some quarters, and there is a substantial professional literature devoted to techniques for squeezing an initial offer out of opposing counsel.

As always, there is considerable wisdom behind the conventional approach, although the fear of going first is usually exaggerated. An initial offer does not need to be a sign of weakness, and the likelihood of a disastrous miscalculation can be virtually eliminated with research and planning. The real benefit from delaying your offer is that it allows you to gather some additional information about your adversary's negotiating posture.

In poker, betting always proceeds in a clockwise direction. Depending on the particular game, the initial bettor might be the person seated to the left of the dealer, or it might be the player with the highest cards showing. In Texas Hold'em, the most popular casino game, a "button" passes from right to left on each hand, indicating the nominal dealer, who is "on the button." The player to the immediate left of the button—said to be "under the gun"—has to act first on every betting round (except the initial round, when the mandatory big and little blinds are posted by the first two players, and the third player starts the betting).

It is a general disadvantage to be seated in the first few seats to the left of the button, called "early position," since you will have to make a decision about betting without getting any information from the other players. You might bet too much, only to be raised by a player to your left who is holding even stronger cards. Or you might bet too little, failing to draw sufficient money into a pot that you are likely to win. In contrast, players in "late position" can get a free preview of your strategy before ever having to make or call a bet. The player on the button is in the best spot of all, able to assess everyone else's possible strengths and weaknesses before making a move.

The early positions simply rotate in poker, so they cannot be avoided. Consequently, skillful players have developed effective strategies when they have to bet first. One approach is to open with a large bet, aimed at causing borderline hands to fold. Bluffing can be particularly effective in early position, since few players would risk making a large bet on anything other than exceptionally strong cards. The reverse technique—called slow playing—involves checking without betting even when holding a good hand. That may embolden others to bet, perhaps foolishly, which will increase the size of the pot.

The point, of course, is that early position comes with a drawback (you have to reveal something to the other players), but even that can be turned to your advantage (you have an opportunity either to bluff or entrap them). While it is always important to obtain information, it can sometimes be just as powerful to dispense it.

LESSON 2: *Taking Their Measure*

What is the most important information in a poker game? You might think it would be the cards—are they rags or the nuts, or somewhere in between? But that would be wrong. In fact, the cards are strictly secondary, really little more than the tableaux against which the game is played. The more important information concerns the players themselves. Are they tight or loose? Can they be bluffed into folding or, better yet, drawn deeply into a hopeless pot? Will they overplay their hands, or are they too timid to go all in? Are they greedy, gullible, patient, or slick? With that sort of information, you can usually win even with bad hands and beat your opponents (in the long run) no matter what they hold—which is why Yardley was fond of saying that he played his opponents, not the cards. Or, to paraphrase Shakespeare, the key is not in our cards, but in ourselves.

You have to understand your opponents—indeed, you have to be able to see through them—in order to win consistently at either poker or law. In his book *Total Poker*, the British journalist David Spanier used a vignette from a film to illustrate why sizing up your adversary is crucial to success. As Spanier explained, "[T]he best film about poker, curiously enough, isn't about poker at all. It's *The Hustler* (1961), which is about pool playing." Evaluating the opposition is a universal skill.

Based on a novel by Walter Tevis, *The Hustler* is the story of Fast Eddie Felson (played by Paul Newman), a young pool player on the make. Eddie is determined to establish his reputation by beating the famed Minnesota Fats, but first he needs to raise a stake by winning some money in a small-town dive. As the film opens, we see Eddie and his pal Charlie entering a slummy bar. The two men begin drinking and playing pool, loudly pretending to be drunk. Eddie loses game after game, attracting attention with his ostentatious complaints, until he somehow manages an impossible three-

cushion shot that ends when the ball runs the length of the
table and into the corner pocket.

"You couldn't play that shot again in a million years," says Charlie.

"I couldn't?" sneers Eddie. "Set 'em up again the way the were before . . . bet ya twenty bucks." Eddie tries the shot again, but he misses badly. In fact, the cue ball flies off the table, as the locals get a good laugh. "Set 'em up again," insists Eddie, but Charlie will have none of it. Stumbling a bit, Eddie angrily slams his money down on the table, demanding to play again. He seems to be challenging Charlie, but of course he is looking around the bar for a mark.

Eddie notices something in the bartender's eye and realizes that he's found his man. He takes out $100, and the barkeep eagerly announces that he will take the bet if no one else will.

"Don't bet any more money on the damn fool shot," warns Charlie, heading for the door. But Eddie is stubborn and overconfident as only a drunk can be. No one can tell him different; he's going to make the shot. The bartender doesn't want to miss his opportunity, so he quickly pulls $100 from the till and lays it on the rail.

With the balls set up and the money in sight, Eddie raises his cue and drops the pretense. With one sinuous motion, he slams home the shot and scoops up the money. Then he races out the door with Charlie, to make their getaway before the stunned barman realizes how thoroughly he has been hustled.

It was nice work, observed Spanier. "Accurate too, because it is the *greed* of the sucker that makes the hustler's skill pay. Without the victim's desire to get rich quick, the hustler couldn't con him along."

Digging for Information

In other words, Eddie's fantastic shot was only incidental. He had to get someone to bet against him if the con were going to work. That required attracting attention and feigning a shaky hand. But most of all, he had to identify a likely mark who could be tempted to bet against him. Recognizing the barman's greed, therefore, was the true heart of the hustle. Without that information, Eddie would have gone home empty-handed no matter how many great shots he made.

The only difference in poker is that everyone knows about the deception. Nonetheless, you still win the most when you can get someone else to smell easy money. You've got the winning hand, but no one can see it—maybe suited face cards in the hole, giving you the nut flush—just as no one in the bar knew that Eddie Felson could make the tricky shot. Now you need someone to bet against you, mistakenly confident that he's got you beaten. You demur a bit; he raises big time on the turn. You just call, setting the hook. He raises again on the river, and this time you go all in. Voila! Just like Fast Eddie, you made someone else's greed work for you.

Now let's revisit Abraham Lincoln's great cross-examination, discussed at some length in the "Diamonds" section. Could it be that Honest Abe and Fast Eddie actually have something in common? Well, they do. Both men knew how to take advantage of an overreaching adversary.

Recall that the key prosecution witness testified that Lincoln's client bit off the victim's nose. But the witness had been birdwatching and was pretty obviously looking the other way during the fight.

"So how can you say that my client bit off his nose?" asked Lincoln, rather bumblingly (though not drunk, like Felson).

"Because I saw him spit it out," retorted the too-eager witness.

But Lincoln was not bumbling at all. He was taking the witness's measure. Finding him greedy and willing to exaggerate, Lincoln moved in for the kill.

"How could you see so clearly at night?" he challenged.

"By the light of the full moon," said the witness. There it was, the equivalent of $100 on the rail, as the witness took the bait.

Just as Fast Eddie slammed home the winning shot, Lincoln produced the *Farmers' Almanac*, proving that it had been a moonless night. Greed observed. Bet won. Case closed.

LESSON 3: *Tells*

Lawyers, judges, and jurors all think that they can read body language as well as Abraham Lincoln, correctly separating the reliable witnesses from the lying scoundrels. There is a near-absolute faith, both professional and popular, that one need only "look the witness in the eye" in order to distinguish honesty from mendacity. This notion is even enshrined in the law of the appellate process, where it is a truism that a trial court's determination of credibility lies beyond all review.

Alas, most research shows that people have only random success at recognizing falsehoods on the basis of demeanor. Studies have consistently found an extremely high error rate in recognizing deception. Observers are wrong between 30% and 60% of the time, and no profession does better than any other. Judges, police officers, social workers, and psychiatrists all tend to score in the same overall range as the general public. One set of tests, for example, was given to police officers, customs examiners, judges, trial lawyers, psychotherapists, and agents of the Federal Bureau of Investigation, Central Intelligence Agency, Drug Enforcement Administration, and Bureau of Alcohol, Tobacco, and Firearms. On average, the subjects, all of whom are expected to be able to weed out deceit in their professional lives, were able to distinguish lying at a rate of 50%—exactly what they would have achieved through random guessing.

Nonetheless, people continue to express great confidence that they can identify verbal and nonverbal conduct that will reveal another's true intentions.

As far as I know, there has been no study of truth detection that specifically included poker players in its sample. Such a survey would be interesting indeed, since poker players are adamant about their proficiency in "reading hands," meaning that they can figure out another player's cards and betting strategy on the basis of unintentional tells. As Sklansky confidently explains, "The ability to read hands is the most important weapon a poker player can have." Mike Caro, who has written an entire book on tells, puts it this way:

> Once you've mastered the basic elements of a winning poker formula, psychology becomes the key ingredient separating break-even players from world-class superstars. The most profitable kind of poker psychology is the ability to read your opponents. Look closely and you'll see opponents giving away the strength of their hands just by their mannerisms. Any mannerism that helps you determine the secrets of an opponent's hand is called a *tell*.

And they are right. There is no doubt that winning poker players can, and do, read their opponents. They can deduce what cards you are holding, figure out whether you are bluffing, and determine the exact move that will cause you to fold (or raise). The stories are legion of poker masters who used three levels of logic and reverse logic to pull off an unlikely bluff or to call, correctly, when the odds seemed disastrous. According to journalist Malcolm Gladwell, certain individuals do seem to be gifted at reading facial expressions, scoring off the charts on various tests. "Most of us aren't very good at spotting it," says Gladwell. "But a handful of people are virtuosos."

What is their secret? Is there really a psychic gift, or perhaps finely honed intuition, that allows poker wizards to see through bluffs and detect deception, exercising a talent that eludes ordinary judges and jurors? And if there is such a skill, how might a trial lawyer acquire it?

For championship-level card players, this skill comes with years of experience, reflection, and insight—not to mention the talent necessary to take advantage of experience, reflection, and insight. Additionally, there are four aspects to the game of poker that allow their abilities to develop. Unfortunately for lawyers, however, only one of these elements has anything approaching a corresponding component in law practice.

The first poker-specific factor is certainty. At the card table, everyone is behaving deceptively, or at least trying to, all of the time. Thus, you never have to determine *whether* someone is attempting to mislead you, but only how and in what manner. Even the most cynical lawyer, however, would have to agree that most witnesses tell the truth most of the time. Different factual accounts are usually the result of failed memories, poor observations, or honest differences of opinion—none of which exist in poker. Thus, distinguishing truth from treachery is immeasurably more difficult in law practice, because you are regularly confronted with both.

In poker, there is only treachery, which makes matters considerably easier. As Anthony Holden says, "Poker is the ultimate monument to the anti-Musketeer code: Every Man For Himself (and be sure, while you're at it, to kick the other guy when he's down)."

The second factor is simplicity. Although there are more than 2.5 million conceivable hands in poker, only three or four will be even remotely possible in any given play. Moreover, the actual question will usually boil down to a simple yes or no. Does your opponent have the cards, or is she bluffing? Thus, the choices are relatively narrow, making them that much easier to read. At trial, in contrast, the scope of possible deception is nearly limitless and hardly ever black and white. Witnesses may testify in various shades of gray about timing, intention, emotion, location, sequence, and other matters of interpretation. The testimony may be a complex jumble of truth, wishful thinking, artful construction, and outright prevarication. Alas, there is nothing binary about it.

Moreover, poker allows the nearly instant validation of one's suspicions. If you think someone is bluffing, based on a tell or some other factor, call her bet and find out. She will have to show her cards, so you can determine immediately whether your suspicion was accurate. In law, there is no reliably similar method of external verification (if there were, we would use it instead of holding a trial). The fact finder will either trust or discount the witness's testimony in what becomes a self-fulfilling analysis. Witnesses are untrustworthy because no one believes them. Yes, witnesses are sometimes caught in lies, or are successfully impeached,

but that is usually because of inherent inconsistencies in
their testimony, not because a lawyer or judge has identified
a valid tell.

Finally, we come to a factor that can be useful to lawyers, although not as might be expected. For all of the talk
of reading hands and watching tells, it turns out that the
single most important determinant is familiarity with your
opponent's playing style. According to Caro:

> Through the analysis of tells we are trying to under-
> stand how players behave and what this reveals about
> their motivation. One of the first steps in discovering
> tells is for a player to develop a sense of the *baseline
> behavioral repertoire* of one's opponents.

The baseline, he continues, needs to be observed over time
so that meaning can be attached to repeated anomalies:

> Again, by cataloging the baseline behavioral reper-
> toire of individual players, one can begin to recognize
> "deviations" from normal pattern[s] and develop a
> second sense, a "feel" for something not being entirely
> correct. In any case a novice poker player, or an expe-
> rienced poker player who enters a new game with
> unknown opponents, should use his calls as a kind
> of behavioral experiment. You have paid not only to
> see a hand, but you have paid to see the *quality* of the
> hand and how it was played.

Bellin explains that he has compiled his own player-
specific "book of tells" over a period of 20 years, cataloging
the tics and giveaways of everyone with whom he has ever
played. "Obviously," he says, "the more familiar you are with
a player, the longer you play against them, the easier they

are to read. Over time, you make notes about their play, and eventually you will be able to predict their actions."

Since poker games move quickly, with as many as 35 hands per hour in Texas Hold'em, there is ample opportunity to observe one's opponents. Familiarity with playing styles can build rapidly, especially in regular games with the same players every week.

Lawyers seldom have this luxury with witnesses, most of whom are not repeat players. Only in fairly unusual circumstances will an attorney have the opportunity to establish a witness's baseline behavioral repertoire. Thus, the interpretation of a witness's mannerisms and demeanor inevitably remain at the level of supposition, if not outright guesswork.

There is a lesson for lawyers in the art of reading poker tells, but it is an ironic one. Lacking the advantages of certainty, simplicity, and validation, lawyers should rely on tells primarily in situations of significant familiarity—rare as those might be.

LESSON 4: *Get What You Need*

Writing in 1977, David Spanier called *The Hustler* the best film ever made about poker. Two decades later, he might have revised his opinion after viewing *Rounders* (1998), which provides a compelling and realistic, if highly dramatized, view of the New York City poker scene. Mike McDermott (played by Matt Damon) is a winsome young law student with a talent for poker. Although he tries to quit playing—keeping his girlfriend happy and forging a new career as a lawyer—he keeps being drawn back into the underground world of basement card rooms, professional gamblers, and thuggish enforcers. The chief of the thugs, and Mike's nemesis, is the Russian émigré Teddy KGB (played by John Malkovich)—a poker genius, ruthless mobster, and operator of the toughest card room in Manhattan. KGB has already busted Mike once at poker, relieving him of his entire bankroll, and he also holds $15,000 of Mike's improvidently acquired, soon-to-be-overdue debt. The climax of the film comes when Mike and KGB face off in a head-to-head, all-night Texas Hold'em game. The stakes are no limit, but they are actually even higher than that for Mike, who will be beaten to a pulp if he cannot win enough to pay off his debt by morning.

For a while, the game goes back and forth. At one point, Mike has enough winnings to erase his debt, but he cannot bring himself to walk away from the table without busting KGB. That appears to be a mistake, as KGB rallies and wins back most of Mike's stack. "Don't worry," the Russian whispers, "soon it will all be over." But then the turning point occurs, on a seemingly improbable hand.

The flop is an A 3 5 rainbow (three different suits). At first, we do not see Mike's hole cards, but we know they are good because he starts to push most of his stack into the middle of the table. But then he spots a tell. Something about KGB's mannerism cautions Mike about betting, so he moves his chips back and simply checks. KGB smiles and moves all in. We haven't seen the pre-flop betting, but at this point it is clear that Mike is going to lose everything if he keeps allowing KGB to steal his blinds. So Mike has to decide whether KGB is bluffing, and it isn't an easy decision. Is this hand worth risking everything?

"I'm laying this down, Teddy," says Mike, flipping over his hand to reveal an ace and a five. "It's the top two pair," he says, "a monster hand, but I'm laying it down. 'Cause you've got two-four, and I'm not going to draw against a made hand."

Teddy goes wild. He had flopped a straight, which should have gotten a lot of action against Mike's two pair. But Mike read him like a book and avoided ruin by folding a great hand. Amarillo Slim would have been proud.

But there is more to the story than that. First, Mike picked up KGB's tell, a crucial piece of information that alerted him to the lurking disaster. Then he had the sense to put KGB on the nut straight, realizing that he couldn't bluff and was unlikely to draw out (only four cards in the deck—another ace or five—could have helped him). Most important, however, Mike decided to show his two pair, letting KGB know that he had the nerve to fold a great hand. "Why the fuck did you lay that down?" fumes KGB, "it should have paid me off." Then he realizes what happened, and he starts throwing things against the wall.

Mike's play was perfect. He got the knowledge he needed and then stopped, realizing it was best to back away for the moment. By showing his monster hand, however, he also set up KGB for future hands. Folding the top two pair was supertight play. Perhaps that meant that Mike would never bluff—a man who would fold aces and fives certainly was not going to bet heavily on rags. Or did it mean the opposite, that Mike was planning to bluff, using the folded monster as a come-on? Mike also established that he could read KGB perfectly, which would make the Russian hesitant to bet heavily, especially on drawing hands, later in the game.

But why did Mike let KGB know that he spotted the tell? Why not keep it a secret to be exploited again and again, for weeks or even months? Mike himself recognized the problem and explained his strategy, "The rule is this: You spot a man's tell, you don't say a fuckin' word. I finally spotted KGB's, and usually I'd've let him go on until he was dead broke. But I don't have that kind of time; I've only got until morning." Besides, "not even Teddy KGB's immune to getting a little rattled."

In other words, Mike wasn't throwing in his hand at all. Realizing that there was "no tomorrow," he made a calculated move to put KGB on tilt, thereby throwing off his game for the rest of the night. Soon enough, we see KGB muttering, "Hanging around, hanging around. The kid's got alligator blood. I can't get the read of him." Mike had the advantage and, this being a Matt Damon film, it worked like a charm.

F. Lee Bailey made a similar play in the O. J. Simpson trial, though with a slightly different endgame. Detective Mark Fuhrman had played a crucial role in the investigation that led to Simpson's arrest, including discovering the bloody glove at the Rockingham estate. Fuhrman's testimony was necessary to complete the chain of custody tying Simpson to the prosecution's strongest physical proof. The defense, however, contended that Fuhrman had carried the glove to Rockingham, planting it there to implicate Simpson. That argument promised to be a tough sell, not least because Fuhrman at first seemed nearly unimpeachable. In Johnnie Cochran's words, he fit everyone's image of an "ideal cop" from central casting.

Well, not quite everyone. More specifically, not F. Lee Bailey. As Cochran put it, Bailey's "trial lawyer's intuition" led him to see a very different side of Fuhrman. "There's something very wrong with this guy's testimony," said Bailey after watching Fuhrman during the preliminary hearing. "I'm telling you there's a flaw in there. And it's a bad one."

Bailey had picked up a tell, and he had a plan for using it on cross-examination.

Again, Cochran described the situation: "Playing on Fuhrman's arrogance and obvious disdain, Bailey danced him around until he stated two things without qualification: He had 'never' spoken the word 'nigger' in the past ten years, and he had 'never' planted evidence."

"Do you use the word 'nigger' in describing people?" Bailey asked.

"No, sir," said Fuhrman politely.

"Have you used that word in the past ten years?"

"Not that I recall."

"Are you therefore saying you have not used that word in the past ten years, Detective Fuhrman?"

"Yes, that is what I'm saying," Fuhrman replied, with somewhat less certainty. The jurors may not have picked up the slight edge in Fuhrman's voice, but Cochran and Bailey heard a small note of caution.

"And you say under oath that you have not addressed any black person as a 'nigger' or spoken about blacks as 'niggers' in the past ten years, Detective Fuhrman?" Bailey demanded.

"That's what I'm saying sir."

"So that anyone who comes to this court and quotes you as using that word in dealing with African Americans would be a liar, would they not, Detective Fuhrman?"

"Yes, they would."

"All of them, correct?" Bailey insisted.

"All of them," Fuhrman replied.

And that, as Cochran would later write, was the "sound of a very large door opening." Almost no one else realized it at the time. Trial commentators were almost unanimous in panning Bailey's cross-examination for failing to "shake" the witness. Fuhrman had calmly denied all accusations, and it would be months before the defense team discovered his taped conversations with screenwriter Laura Hart McKinney.

It seemed as though Bailey had laid down his hand, giving up on a promising line of questioning without scoring many points. Fuhrman himself, of course, knew differently. He knew that he had been tape recorded repeatedly using the racial slur, and he had to worry about whether Simpson's lawyers had the tapes. Perhaps even more significantly, Bailey was not the only one who correctly read the tells. "I could tell by the way he twisted around in his seat and clenched his hands in his lap, that he was lying," the jury foreperson would say after the trial. Fuhrman's repeated lies about the n-word (he was later convicted of perjury, following the testimony of Laura McKinney) infected the rest of his testimony, fatally undermining his insistence that he had never planted evidence. F. Lee Bailey's seeming lay down, just like Matt Damon's, did its work and then some.

LESSON 5: *True Lies*

The most reliable tells are the involuntary ones—mannerisms, habits, nods, and speech patterns—over which the players themselves have no control (and usually do not even know about). According to Andy Bellin, these quirks are the result of a conflict between childhood morality ("stand up straight and tell the truth") and poker's demand for constant deception. Poker is one of the rare social situations in which lying, or at least misrepresentation, is acceptable or even encouraged. Consequently, most casual players experience an emotional reaction to deceit, typically something akin to a guilty thrill, that can produce anything from a smile to a blink to a heavily furrowed brow. Superior players have learned to suppress these reactions—the fabled "poker face"—as well as to read them in others. They also frequently hide their expressions behind broad-brimmed hats and sunglasses, tactics that are not available in courtrooms.

It is easy enough to tell when someone is reacting to his own cards (and yours). Shaking hands, furtive glances, anguished sighs, clenched fists, and shoulder shrugs are all impossible to miss at the card table. But what do they mean? How should they be interpreted? Does a sweaty brow mean that your opponent hit the nut flush and hopes that you will call? Or does it mean that he missed his hand on the river and hopes that you will fold? He would be nervous, perhaps equally nervous, in either case, so there is no absolute formula for interpreting an adversary's body language.

Nonetheless, Mike Caro believes that certain tells are relatively consistent from player to player, conveying the same information about their hands. For example, Caro cautions that a "suddenly shaking hand" almost always indicates that your opponent has great cards and is not bluffing. This is somewhat counterintuitive—you would probably think that a trembling hand is the sign of a nervous bluffer—and therefore somewhat contrary to Bellin's observation about morality and deceit.

But Caro makes a good case. Bluffers, he says, "bolster themselves and often become rigid. They don't allow themselves to shake, because they're afraid the shaking would make you suspicious and prompt you to call." Conversely, a shaking hand indicates the release of tension "that comes automatically when the suspense ends." A player who has made a big hand—often a truly monumental hand—expects to win, and his suddenly shaking hand "signals the happy ending to drama." Conversely, a player who is holding his breath *is* probably bluffing, according to Caro. Players backing weak hands are afraid of calling attention to themselves, so they attempt to become less noticeable by freezing, and sometimes they even stop breathing. Consequently, you should be inclined to fold against a hand trembler and call or raise a breath holder.

This seems like sound advice, and Caro himself has certainly been successful as a player, teacher, and maven. Most important, he never claims to be able to interpret tells with 100% accuracy. "A tell is just another factor to consider," he says, "and it needs to be weighed along with all other factors." What sort of player are you facing? How has she behaved on past hands? Who else is at the table? What are the pot odds? And how large are the stakes? Ultimately, you will have to fold, call, or raise on every hand, and that will give you an opportunity to validate (or discount) any tells you have tentatively identified. If the bet is small enough, go ahead and call the player holding her breath (or better yet, wait for someone else to call her), and you will quickly find out whether she is bluffing.

Granting that Mike Caro is an astute observer and shrewd commentator, lawyers still have to wonder what it means when a witness's hand starts shaking. Is it a sign of deception or just an emotional release? Is he hiding something, or is he merely nervous about speaking in public? Alas, it is impossible to generalize. Trembling hands (or baited breath, for that matter) must mean something, but it is likely to be different for every witness.

Even if there is no universal key to a witness's body language, there *are* a number of commonly held perceptions (or perhaps misperceptions) about demeanor and truthfulness. Shaking hands and shifting posture, for example, will almost always be interpreted as signs of deceit. Jurors, and judges too, regularly report that they disbelieved witnesses who appeared nervous or shifty, even though, per Caro, we know that the exact opposite might be the case. An earnest witness may be overly concerned about her appearance—more so than a practiced liar—and therefore appear jittery or uptight.

There are other verbal and nonverbal cues that are frequently assumed to indicate deceit, although none of them ever have been actually correlated with truth or falsity. These include speech patterns such as unnaturally short or clipped answers, hesitation and stammering, verbal tics ("uhh, well, let's see, umm"), garbled or fragmentary language, voice tremors, and constant self-reference ("to be perfectly honest"). A witness's attitude can also make a difference. Anger, self-righteousness, or aggressiveness—even when justified by the circumstances—will often be construed as dishonesty. So will a completely flat affect or lack of emotion, so a perfect poker face is actually a disadvantage on the witness stand. When it comes to pure body language, shaking hands and shifting posture can be deadly to a witness. The other most frequently perceived indicators of deceit include rapid blinking, lack of eye contact, grinning, folded arms, and overactive hand gestures.

In poker, you always want your opponents to doubt your motives. If they misinterpret your tells, so much the better. Trial work, of course, is just the opposite, especially when it comes to witnesses. They have to tell the truth and, nearly as

important, they have to look like they are telling the truth.
Recognizing the power of tells, and the pitfalls, should cause
lawyers to redouble their efforts at witness preparation.

LESSON 6: *That's Acting*

In addition to involuntary (or subconscious) tells, there are
also many "acted" tells—intentional behaviors that are meant
to be deceptive, but which can actually be quite transparent
to the trained eye. In most cases, they are derivative of the
basic poker strategy to show strength when weak and weakness when strong. Thus, an opponent who is conspicuously
attempting to appear weak ("oh, please don't call my bet")
might be holding the nuts, and a blustering player ("do yourself a favor and fold") may well be bluffing. These are stories nearly as old as literature itself. Think of Atlas and the
golden apples, or Brer Rabbit and the briar patch, or Tom
Sawyer and the whitewashed fence.

Of course, it is not always that simple. Only the most
naive player would attempt to fool you so blatantly. So a
boast like "do yourself a favor and fold" might turn out to
be an example of second-level strategy: a strong player faking
a bluff, hoping that you will misinterpret his hand and call
rather than fold. An intricate move, indeed.

Consequently, the first challenge is to determine when
your opponent is acting. Mike Caro offers this advice: "It's
probably an act if the player has reason to believe you might
be observing a specific mannerism *and* it is of obvious value
to him that your conclusion is wrong." Importantly, as Caro
points out, both conditions are necessary. Your opponent
must believe you are watching, *and* your decision must mat-

ter to him. Thus, a novice who folds his cards out of turn is probably not acting. He may know that you are watching, but your decision does not matter because he has no intention of staying in the hand. On the other hand, a seasoned pro who starts to fold out of turn is likely trying to get you to stay in the pot—by indicating that there will be less competition—but in reality is planning to raise.

Even when you are certain that your opponent is acting, you still have to decide whether you are seeing first- or second-level deception. Is it the old weak-when-strong ploy, or is it a bit of more sophisticated reverse psychology? The trick, as Caro puts it, is the Great Law of Tells: Decide what your opponents want you to do, and then disappoint them. This is not as hard as it might seem. As Steven Seagal has proven time and again, bad acting usually looks like, well, bad acting—and most card players are not even that good.

Fortunately, it turns out that there are some acted tells that can be usefully identified in most situations. For example, overt disinterest is almost always the sign of a strong hand. A player staring away from the pot is trying to avoid drawing attention to herself. She wants you to think that she is not following the action, that she has no particular plan, and of course, that she is not trying to set you up for a big score. By the same token, a player who shrugs or sighs, or expresses reluctance when betting, is probably trying to disguise a powerful hand. As Caro puts it, "Why would players go out of their way to convey sadness and make you suspicious if they didn't want you to call?"

On the other hand, a player who attempts to stare you down, or who aggressively pitches his chips into the pot, is trying to appear confident, which probably means a bluff. True, an outstanding player might rudely "splash" the pot as a feigned bluff, trying to keep you in the game because he has a monster hand. But most players, even good ones, are too insecure to try a move like that, afraid that they will end up scaring you away. It is safer to bet quietly, sliding the chips into the pot as though it is no big deal. Nice and easy, let's keep playing.

Most lawyers are mediocre actors, at best. As with card players, then, feigned indifference is a reliable sign of active interest. At a deposition, for example, everyone knows that a preface such as "by the way" or "for the sake of curiosity" can only mean that the lawyer is zeroing in on something truly important. An expression of surprise may sometimes be sincere, especially if it is an unforced exclamation ("What!"), but otherwise it is usually an attempt to get a well-prepared witness to expand on a damaging answer.

The biggest tip-offs, of course, come in settlement discussions. The more a lawyer professes eagerness to bring a case to trial, the harder he is trying to shake out an early settlement offer. And you will need an entire salt shaker when you hear a lawyer say something like, "My client will never settle, but I can do my best to convince him." Sure, counselor, whatever you say. Just don't splash the pot.

LESSON 7: *Calling Bias*

Almost no one sits down at the card table planning to throw away 50 or 100 hands in a row. Even Herbert Yardley's acolytes, the tightest of all players, want to see some action and win some pots. While they might be disciplined enough to refrain from raising with weak hands, many will be hoping to spot bluffers, thinking they can call a few bets to keep others from stealing the pot. In other words, they want to be able to call, no matter how bad their cards. More significantly, they will be looking for reasons to call, real or imaginary. Mike Caro refers to this as the "calling reflex," explaining that poor-to-mediocre players are generally biased against folding and in favor of calling bets, even if they have to invent reasons for doing so. The best players are aware of the reflex and compensate for it, but less-capable opponents cannot help themselves, if you know how to take advantage of their weaknesses.

According to Caro, you are more likely to be called when you are animated, say, shifting in your chair or playing with your coffee mug. Some of your opponents will be inclined to construe virtually any movement as a tell, and because they are disposed to call in the first place, they will assume that the tell indicates a bluff. As Caro explains, "They're a little bit like snakes, predisposed to strike at the slightest move. Except they're poker opponents, predisposed to call for the slightest reason."

This insight can give you a significant advantage when you are holding a strong hand and want to keep other players in the pot. When you sense that someone is about to fold, do something. Anything. Swallow hard, knock over some chips, shuffle your hole cards, stretch your arms. Someone otherwise reluctant to fold just might conclude that you've given away a bluff and decide not to throw away his hand just yet. Even if it doesn't work, well, you haven't lost anything, because your opponent was going to fold in the first place.

In any event, it is important to realize that the calling bias causes many players to use tells incorrectly. They conjure up imaginary tells that prompt them to call, while ignoring the actual tells that should have prompted them to fold.

There are witnesses who react in essentially the same way, especially when they are highly invested in the outcome of the litigation. As with card players, almost no one walks into the deposition room, much less the courtroom, planning to keep quiet about the justice of her cause. Witnesses want to tell the story. They want to explain and justify themselves. They want to convince everyone in sight—including opposing counsel—that they are firmly in the right. Let's call this the "answering bias." It can provide you with a powerful tool.

Most witnesses, to be sure, have been cautioned to avoid loose talk, just as most poker players are well aware of the advantages of tight play. But often they cannot help themselves. They will be looking for reasons—inventing reasons—to give in to their reflexes and start talking. It would be unfair to call them snakes, since they mostly want to tell their versions of the truth, but they will pretty much react to anything that seems like a moving target.

Did any witness ever suffer a greater talking bias, to worse effect, than President William Jefferson Clinton? A Yale-educated lawyer, Rhodes scholar, former constitutional law professor, and Arkansas attorney general—not to mention consummate politician and debater—he understood the litigation process far better than most other witnesses. In the crucible of cross-examination, however, when brevity could have been the soul of his defense, he simply could not restrain himself.

Clinton's moment of truth came on August 17, 1998, when he appeared for questioning before a grand jury empaneled by Special Counsel Kenneth Starr. His earlier deposition testimony in the Paula Jones case had just been a warm-up, as he had relatively little difficulty deflecting the inartful questions of Jones's inept lawyers. But now he was facing experienced prosecutors, armed with the power of indictment, who knew how to exploit every opening and seize the slightest lead.

The president's lawyers had obviously counseled him that short answers were essential, and at first it seemed that he understood. Within the first few minutes of the interrogation, he read a prepared statement explaining that he would limit most of his answers "because of privacy considerations affecting my family . . . and in an effort to preserve the dignity of the office I hold." The prosecutor appeared to assent, but it was not long before Clinton was disastrously (from his perspective) expanding on his responses.

Even when questions often called for simple "yes" or "no" answers, Clinton would elaborate at great length, often adding details that would come back to haunt him. At one point—perhaps sincerely, perhaps as a ploy—the prosecutor attempted to point out that Clinton's already-extensive answer was quite sufficient.

"With all respect, Mister . . . ," he said.

"Now let me finish," Clinton interrupted. "I mean, you brought this up."

From that point onward, the prosecutors were content to allow Clinton to continue his stream-of-conscious narrative. In fact, they often encouraged him. It was not long before Clinton committed his most memorable faux pas.

The prosecutor was pursuing a line of questioning about events in the Jones case. During the president's deposition, Clinton's lawyer had asserted that "there is absolutely no sex [with Monica Lewinsky] of any kind in any manner, shape or form with President Clinton."

"That statement is a completely false statement," asked the prosecutor. "Is that correct?"

"It depends on what the meaning of the word 'is' is," the president famously replied. "If 'is' means is and never has been . . . that is one thing. If it means there is none, that was a completely true statement."

The tortured equivocation was quite unnecessary. Clinton could just as easily have answered "yes" or "no," neither of which would have damaged him as much as the slippery explanation.

Clinton's extensive evasions before the grand jury became the basis for one of the articles of impeachment voted by the House of Representatives. And while he was not convicted before the Senate on any of the four counts, Clinton's second term was severely compromised by the contentious proceeding (not to mention Al Gore's chances in the 2000 election).

The Clinton administration was a time of unparalleled peace and prosperity, for which Clinton himself may justly claim great credit. Nonetheless, his detractors will always be able to insist that his legacy is best defined by the eponymous adjective "Clintonian," thanks to his eager haggling over the definition of the word *is*.

LESSON 8: *Paying Attention*

The only way to read your opponents is by paying close attention to them at every opportunity. Do not tune out or leave the table when you have folded a hand. Instead, keep an eye on the active players and try to pick up their general habits and characteristics. Watch their moves and interactions, how they behave when bluffing or betting for value, how carefully they select their hands, whether they can be intimidated, who plays a tight game, and who is likely to steam.

When you are in the game, it is even more important to watch your opponents, trying to put each one on a particular hand. Their bets, especially their opening bets, will tell part of the story. A large pre-flop raise, for example, usually represents either a high pair or high suited connectors. But of course, you will have to be alert for specific tells that indicate bluffing or semi-bluffing. This is especially true on the flop, when everyone will be watching the cards to see whether they have improved their hands.

Everyone but you, that is.

There is no reason to look at the cards as they fall on the table. They are not going anywhere, and staring at them won't do you any good. Instead, you should be watching your opponents as they watch the flop. You will never get a better read on their reactions. In the half-moment before they adjust their responses, you may be able to tell whether the flop helps or disappoints them, as eyes widen, breaths quicken, brows furrow, muscles relax, or teeth clench.

Mike Caro has even identified a couple of common tells that are unique to the flop. Players who immediately look at their chips are telling you (involuntarily) that they liked the flop and are planning to bet. Often, they will catch themselves and look quickly away, which makes the tell even more reliable. Players who initially stare at the cards, however, probably got no help but are looking more closely just to make sure. Continued staring and smiling, however, indicates bluffing, as the grinner wants you to think that he made a big hand.

But whatever the signals, the key is to be on the alert for them. And that means watching the people instead of the cards.

Lawyers often have the same problem during witness examinations. They tend to keep their eyes on their notes or outlines, rather than on their witnesses. While it helps to think carefully about the next question, it helps even more to listen closely to the witness's answers, which may provide a crucial insight or an opening for a devastating follow-up.

One such missed opportunity occurred in the trial of Nicola Sacco and Bartolomeo Vanzetti in 1921. The two Italian anarchists were charged with murder following the armed robbery of a factory payroll truck in South Braintree, Massachusetts. The evidence against them was slim, and many believed that they were being persecuted for their immigrant status and radical beliefs. Nonetheless, they were convicted and sentenced to death, largely on the evidence of a police ballistics expert who tied Sacco to the murder weapon.

The prosecution witness, William Proctor, testified at length on direct examination about bullet identification. Specifically, he compared a bullet taken from the body of the dead security guard to a Colt pistol that was seized from Sacco when he was arrested. Then came the hammer:

Q: Have you an opinion as to whether bullet three was fired from the Colt Automatic which is in evidence?

A: I have.

Q: And what is your opinion?

A: My opinion is that it is consistent with being fired by that pistol.

"That pistol," of course, was Sacco's, and the testimony seemed to seal his fate. Defense counsel Jeremiah McAnarney was capable and extremely well prepared. He launched into a stinging cross-examination of Proctor, questioning the witness's experience and challenging his judgment on the manufacture of guns, the location and meaning of the "lands and grooves" on the various bullets, and the possible existence of a different murder weapon. Whenever Proctor strayed or attempted to explain an answer, McAnarney brought him quickly back to heel. The defense lawyer had a clear agenda for the cross-examination, and he intended to stick to it.

Perhaps because he was so well prepared, McAnarney did not catch the ambiguity in Proctor's direct examination, testifying only that the murder bullet was "consistent" with being fired from Sacco's pistol. In other words, he could not really say whether it came from Sacco's revolver or from another Colt automatic of like caliber.

In any event, the crucial discrepancy was not raised on cross-examination nor mentioned during defense counsel's lengthy final argument. The case went to the jury, which deliberated for one day. The defendants were convicted and condemned to die.

Following the convictions, however, defense lawyers scoured the record for error and discovered Proctor's hedged testimony. Using the discrepancy in support of a motion for a new trial, they called Proctor back to the witness stand. He admitted that he used the indeterminate phrase "consistent with" by prearrangement with the prosecution, so that the jury might conclude that Sacco's gun had been proven to be the murder weapon.

These new facts might have raised a reasonable doubt among the jurors, especially if the cross-examination of Proctor had compelled him to recant his direct testimony. But the hostile trial judge was unmoved. He denied the motion for a new trial, and his ruling was upheld by the higher courts. Many thoughtful Americans, including future Supreme Court justice Felix Frankfurter, believed that the defendants were not guilty. Despite massive protests and widespread public support, however, Sacco and Vanzetti were electrocuted on August 23, 1927.

LESSON 9: *Reading Value*

In the Sacco and Vanzetti case, Proctor's ballistics testimony was a semi-bluff. He did not actually have all the cards, but he represented a made hand and got away with it when McAnarney failed to fully cross-examine him. It is easy to criticize the defense lawyer after the fact, especially if he simply missed the ambiguity in the witness's testimony. But there is another possibility as well.

Perhaps McAnarney realized that Proctor was hedging his testimony and consciously chose not to pursue the point. After all, it could have been a setup. Police experts are tricky witnesses to cross-examine (and always have been). They are usually quite ready to frustrate defense lawyers, especially when they venture into unfamiliar territory. At the very least, McAnarney would have had to worry about challenging Proctor, wondering whether the witness was prepared with a pat explanation of why "consistent" really meant "guilty." It would have been risky to ask the witness to explain, so perhaps defense counsel simply determined that discretion was the better part of valor.

In other words, McAnarney had to decide—on the spot—whether Proctor was bluffing or betting for value, which would in turn determine whether defense counsel should raise or fold. That is always a complicated read, and a mistake can be devastating.

David Sklansky provides one way of figuring out whether your adversary is betting for value:

> When an opponent bets in a situation where he is sure you are going to call, he is not bluffing. . . . If you create the impression—by the way you have played your hand, by the look of your board, by the action you have put in the pot, or even by artificial means—that you are going to call a bet, an opponent who bets is betting for value.

It basically boils down to a single proposition: Only an idiot would bluff when he believes that you intend to call. So if you have been betting strongly all the way, representing a made hand, your opponent's monster raise on the river is almost certainly a bet for value.

Recall Oscar Wilde's first trial in 1895. The Marquess of Queensberry had called Wilde a "posing sodomite," and Wilde opened the betting by filing a complaint for criminal libel. In response, Queensberry filed a "plea of justification," including the claim that Wilde had been involved in sexual activity with six or more "rent boys." That was a huge raise in the stakes, as the case was no longer simply about Wilde's outré lifestyle and extravagant persona. Instead, it promised to be a case about very specific acts, each of which happened to constitute a "crime against nature" and therefore

an imprisonable felony. Was Queensberry bluffing, or was
he betting for value? Was he simply trying to scare Wilde
into dropping the case, or would he be able to establish his
defense and send Wilde himself to jail?

Initially, it seems that Wilde (or his lawyer, or both) did
not believe that Queensberry had the goods. They refused
to fold the libel case, and Wilde even took the stand to deny
under oath that he had ever engaged in "gross indecency."
But Queensberry came out swinging (so to speak, and to mix
a metaphor). Edward Carson, on Queensberry's behalf, cross-
examined Wilde thoroughly, vigorously, and in excruciating
detail. He asked question after question, with names, dates,
places, circumstances, and even the descriptions of various
sexual acts (a bold move in Victorian England).

Yes, Carson might have been bluffing. It was not at all
certain that any of the rent boys were actually willing to testify against Wilde. Then again, he might have been holding
a made hand, with firm commitments from one or more of
the young men, perhaps motivated by anger at Wilde or the
hope of leniency from the police. Wilde's lawyer, the highly
respected Sir Edward Clarke, former solicitor general of
England, had to decide what to do.

For a while, it appears that Clarke managed to persuade
himself that Queensberry was bluffing. Before agreeing to
take the case, after all, Clarke had made Wilde swear "on his
honor as an English gentleman" that he had never engaged
in "sodomitical" behavior. Slowly, however, it must have
dawned on Clarke that Wilde was actually an Irishman, a
small fact that the poet had earlier neglected to point out.

In any event, the Queensberry side never faltered or hesitated. And neither did Wilde, dishing out indignant deni-
als, rapier-like witticisms, and memorable bon mots as rap-

idly as Carson could throw accusations. It may have been Carson's tenacity that most of all persuaded Clarke to throw in his hand. Wilde, indeed, had indicated that he was willing to fight to the finish, and yet the cross-examiner would not relent. Only a fool would keep bluffing in those circumstances. And while it is true that Queensberry was a bully and a buffoon, Edward Carson, the cross-examiner, most clearly was not.

At a break in the proceedings, Clarke counseled his client that there was no way to win the libel action. Indeed, the only hope of avoiding a follow-up prosecution, for perjury if not sodomy, was to abandon the case.

So Oscar Wilde threw in the towel (another unavoidable boxing metaphor) and dismissed his suit. That bought him sufficient time to arrange an escape to Paris while Queensberry attempted to persuade Her Majesty's government to prosecute Wilde (as Clarke had feared). For unfathomable reasons, however, Wilde continued his own bluff. He inexplicably stayed in London and soon enough found himself in the prisoner's dock, charged with multiple counts of sodomy. The rent boys were indeed willing to testify, or were coerced into it, and Wilde was convicted and sentenced to two years at hard labor in Reading Gaol.

And that brings us back to Sacco and Vanzetti. Did their defense lawyer simply blunder in his inflexible and therefore incomplete cross-examination of the prosecution ballistics expert, or did he accurately read the witness, recognizing that he was betting for value? Alas, the record indicates the former. While it is conceivable that McAnarney might have made a strategic decision not to cross-examine Proctor about the gap in his testimony—whether the bullet was fired from Sacco's gun or merely "consistent"—that cannot

explain why he failed to refer to it during his final argument.
Once Proctor was no longer on the stand, there could be no
fear that he would explain away the problem in his direct testimony. Thus, there was nothing to keep McAnarney from
hammering away at it, explaining to the jury that a merely
consistent bullet left lots of room for reasonable doubt. But
McAnarney did not so much as allude to the inconsistency,
which strongly suggests that he never noticed it—until it was
too late.

LESSON 10: *Total Recall*

Card games such as bridge and blackjack require exceptional powers of immediate recall, because accurate card
counting is essential to correct play. That sort of memo-
rization is relatively unimportant in poker. In seven-card
stud (and five-card stud, to the extent that it is still played),
you need to remember the cards that have been folded so
that you can accurately count the remaining outs. Other
than that, however, card counting is not really necessary.
In Texas Hold'em, as well as in five-card draw, you can
always see all of the relevant cards, so there is nothing to
remember.

There is a different sort of memory, however, that is crucial in poker—the recall of specific hands. Although poker
is a game of infinite complexity and finesse, there are many
situations that are repeated again and again. Studying these
situations can provide a tremendous advantage to a skilled
player. Impressive moves may appear to be instinctive, but in
fact they are often the result of careful study and long-term
planning. Doyle Brunson explains it this way:

Digging for Information

Whenever I use the word "feel," you should understand it's not some extra-sensory power that I have.
It's just that I recall something that happened previously. Even though I might not consciously do it, I
can often recall if this same play or something close
to it came up in the past, and what the player did or
what somebody else did. So, many times I get a feeling
that he's bluffing or that I can make a play and get the
pot. But actually my subconscious mind is reasoning
it all out.

In the film *Rounders*, for example, we see Mike McDermott
studying a videotape of Johnny Chan playing Erik Seidel in
the final hand at the 1988 World Series of Poker. Chan had
flopped the nut straight, an unbeatable hand, but he slow
played it all the way. Checking from the flop to the river,
Chan suckered Seidel into betting all of his chips and won
the world championship. Mike played and replayed the tape,
watching Chan's demeanor and Seidel's reactions. "Johnny
fuckin' Chan," says Mike admiringly. He knew his opponent
well enough to reel him in.

Later, in his dramatic head-to-head showdown with
Teddy KGB, Mike is getting dangerously low on chips when
he flops the nut straight. The board shows 6♦ 7♠ 10♥, with
Mike holding 8♠ 9♠ in the hole. He checks to KGB, who
reacts just as Mike hoped. "You on a draw, Mike?" he sneers,
and bets $2,000.

"All right, I'll gamble," says Mike, calling the bet. The turn
is a useless card (a "blank"), and Mike checks again, looking
increasingly worried. KGB splashes $4,400 into the pot, and
Mike reluctantly calls. "Or else I won't respect myself in the
morning," he says.

"In the morning," replies KGB, "respect is all you will have left."

The river is another blank. Mike checks as before, and KGB keeps splashing. "You can't believe what fell," he taunts, "your hopes down the fucking drain." Moving all in, he says, "That card couldn't have helped you. Bet it all."

"You're right," says Mike, cracking a faint smile. "It didn't help me. I flopped the nut straight." He pushes his chips in and shows his cards, and KGB goes wild with anger and frustration.

Virtually channeling Johnny Chan, Mike busted KGB and won the day. As Doyle Brunson might explain, Mike had a feel for the hand, meaning that he recalled Johnny Chan's play in like circumstances and coolly emulated the master. It might seem like a pat ending, but it is not farfetched at all. It made sense for Mike to make a point of remembering Chan's approach, assuming that he would have his own opportunity to use it later. True, the odds against flopping a straight are 254 to 1, and the odds of flopping the nut straight are somewhat worse. But Mike could realistically hope to draw such a hand now and then—especially playing all-night sessions at the rate of 35 hands per hour. So he knew that his plans—and recollection—could some day pay off.

Litigation is nowhere nearly as repetitive as poker, and it moves much more slowly. Still, a good memory is obviously important to a trial lawyer, as is a feel for particular situations.

On the afternoon of March 25, 1911, there was a terrible fire in the Asch Building near Washington Square in Manhattan. The Triangle Shirtwaist Company occupied the top three floors of the building, with hundreds of immigrant women, many of them teenagers, employed in the ninth-floor cutting room. As smoke and flames filled the factory, they rushed for the exits, only to find the stairways inadequate and some of the doors locked. Trapped in a suffocating inferno, 146 people would die, nearly all of them young women—some from burns, some from asphyxiation, and some from injuries suffered when they frantically jumped from the windows. Meanwhile, the executives on the tenth floor calmly walked up to the building's rooftop, where they were later rescued without incident.

The citizens of New York were outraged that so many young lives had been lost so needlessly. There was an insistent demand for prosecution, and within two weeks the owners of the factory were indicted for manslaughter. Specifically, it was charged that they had locked the exit doors on the ninth floor in order to prevent their employees from sneaking out and stealing goods. That was a violation of the labor code, if proven, and the resulting deaths would therefore amount to manslaughter.

Numerous prosecution witnesses testified that the door on the Washington Place side of the building had been locked or inoperable, leading to the deaths of women who were caught, or even crushed, as they vainly tried to open it. Specifically, the prosecutors contended that a girl named Margaret Schwartz had died when she was trapped against the Washington Place door.

Kate Alterman, one of Schwartz's friends and coworkers, was an especially effective witness. Speaking with a thick Yiddish accent, Kate described the horrors of that afternoon:

> I noticed someone, a whole crowd around the door and I saw Bernstein, the manager's brother trying to open the door, and there was Margaret near him. Ber-

nstein tried the door, he couldn't open it and then Margaret began to open the door. I take her on one side I pushed her on the side and I said, "Wait, I will open that door." I tried, pulled the handle in and out, all ways—and I couldn't open it. She pushed me on the other side, got hold of the handle and then she tried. And then I saw her bending down on her knees, and her hair was loose, and the trail of her dress was a little far from her, and then a big smoke came and I couldn't see. I just know it was Margaret, and I said, "Margaret," and she didn't reply. I left Margaret, I turned my head on the side, and I noticed the trail of her dress and the ends of her hair begin to burn.

Between the machines and between the examining tables, I noticed afterwards on the other side, near the Washington side windows, Bernstein, the manager's brother, throwing around like a wildcat at the window, and he was chasing his head out of the window, and pull himself back. He wanted to jump, I suppose, but he was afraid. And then I saw the flames cover him. I noticed on the Greene street side someone else fell down on the floor and the flames cover him.

The whole door was a red curtain of fire. A young lady came and she began to pull me in the back of my dress and she wouldn't let me in. I kicked her with my foot and I don't know what became of her. I ran out through the Greene street side door, right through the flames on to the roof.

The courtroom was transfixed, but defense lawyer Max Steuer thought he'd heard something odd in Alterman's testimony. Abandoning all of the rules of cross-examination, he asked her to repeat the story. She told it again, and this time Steuer knew there was something wrong. Even without the aid of a transcript, he realized there had been a slight change in Alterman's wording, so he asked her about the flames.

She quickly corrected herself. It was "like a red curtain."

"And how was Bernstein acting?" came the next question.

"Like a wildcat," Alterman told him.

"You left that out the second time?" asked Steuer. "You did leave that out, didn't you, just now?" Then he asked her to tell the story again.

Alterman obliged, this time including the reference to Bernstein acting like a "wildcat" and the "red curtain" of flames.

Now Steuer was certain that Alterman had been coached and had memorized her testimony. But rather than confront her, he slow played his hand:

Q: You never spoke to anybody about what you were going to tell us when you came here, did you?

A: No, sir.

Q: And you didn't study the words in which you would tell it?

A: No, sir.

The naive Kate Alterman had been led into an obvious lie, which was far more damaging to her credibility than the truth, that she had planned her statement with the prosecutors. But Max Steuer was not finished yet. He asked her to tell the story yet again. And so she did, with the same result.

It took a powerful memory for Max Steuer to replay Kate Alterman's testimony word for word, even as he devised his cross-examination. But the strategy apparently worked. After

only two hours of deliberation, the jury acquitted the defendants of all charges.

LESSON 11: *The Unexpected*

Sometimes you will find memorable information when you
least expect it.

Following the publication of *The American Black Chamber* in 1931, Herbert Yardley found himself ostracized in
the American intelligence community. Within a few years,
however, he managed to find suitable employment in Asia,
hired by the Chinese government to organize its intelligence
service. Marked as an enemy by the Japanese, Yardley was
forced to work under cover to avoid recognition and possible assassination.

Along with his translator, Ling Fan, Yardley was sent to
Chungking in China's interior where, safe from the invading
Japanese, he was tasked with developing a cryptographic program for the interception of Japanese military dispatches. As
the administrative center of the Chinese government, Chungking attracted a constellation of "foreign advisors, corre-
spondents, businessmen, diplomats, as well as spies, crooks,
whores and expatriates." Conditions were austere, with little
in the way of luxury or entertainment, but there was a permanent poker game at the Chungking Hostel that attracted
participants of every nationality and description. Yardley
made it his second home, and he endeavored to teach Ling
Fan the secrets of the game.

One night, the game was joined by a young German, sup-
posedly a refugee from Nazi tyranny. Yardley described him
as "about thirty, a big blond, soft spoken, and he carried him-

self like a soldier." He was traveling on a forged Honduran passport, which hardly distinguished him from most of the Europeans in Chungking.

The game progressed uneventfully until the German and Ling Fan went head to head in a big hand of seven-card stud. After five cards had been dealt—two down, three up—the German bet US$500, which was a small fortune in wartime China. Ling called nervously; he was on a draw and had not yet made his hand. There was even more betting on the sixth card.

"What's the Hong Kong rate of exchange?" whispered the German.

"About four to one," answered a pilot who was sitting out the hand.

"I bet US$1,000," said the German, slapping down 2,000 Hong Kong dollars and then pulling out his bulging wallet. He peeled off five U.S. hundred-dollar bills and threw them into the pot.

It was obvious to Yardley that Ling still had not made his hand, but the translator warily threw his last $1,000 into the pot. Then came the seventh card, face down.

Without even looking at his last hole card, the German reached for his wallet and began counting out a sheaf of hundred-dollar U.S. bills.

"I bet $2,000 gold," he said with no inflection.

Ling turned to Yardley. "Advisor," he said, "you got any money?"

Realizing that Ling must have made his hand on the last card, Yardley unbuttoned his trousers and removed his money belt, slipping 20 hundred-dollar bills to his friend. Sure enough, Ling had the German beat. He gathered the money and smiled.

Yardley, however, was not happy. He took Ling by the arm and hurried him away from the table, indicating that they should remain silent about what had just happened. Back at their quarters, Yardley examined the German's U.S. currency, determining that the serial numbers began with E048936642Y and ended with E048936965Y.

"The serial numbers indicate the German had over $30,000 gold in his purse," exclaimed Yardley, "that is, if the numbers run consecutively."

"They do," said the observant Ling. "The first five bills he took from the left side of his wallet, the next 20 he took from the right."

"That's too much money for a refugee to be carrying around," said Yardley. "He's a squarehead Nazi agent."

Suspecting that the spy would also have a hidden radio transmitter, Yardley moved some of his equipment near the German's room in the hostel. Sure enough, he was able to begin intercepting thinly coded messages. Yardley hoped to maintain the intercepts until he could locate the German's confederates, but his Chinese superiors were unwilling to let the spy stay at his work. They arrested him almost immediately but allowed Yardley to conduct the interrogation. At first, the German was intransigent, but Yardley explained that he was facing execution and promised to protect him if he confessed. That shook loose part of the story, and the application of sodium amytal (illegal even then in the United States, but freely usable in wartime China) obtained the rest.[1]

---

[1] According to Yardley, sodium amytal was developed at Northwestern University, where I have taught for over thirty years. Just thought I'd point that out.

The German was an advance agent in a plot to kidnap and perhaps even kill Generalissimo Chiang Kai-shek. Yardley's keen eye and poker savvy had unmasked an enemy operation that might have altered the course of World War II (at least in his telling).

There is no truly comparable story about litigation. A lawyer on television might discover a sinister spy ring in the course of a trial, or stumble across the real murderer during cross-examination, but that sort of thing does not happen in real life. Perhaps the closest parallel occurred in the Senate Watergate hearings of 1973, when White House appointments secretary Alexander Butterfield stunned the investigating committee by revealing the existence of President Richard Nixon's secret audiotapes. The resulting legal struggle over access to the tapes and the subsequent discovery of a mysterious 18-minute gap led to the downfall of the Nixon presidency.

The lesson is clear. Stay alert.

LESSON 12: *Local Rules*

As painfully obvious as it may seem, it is essential for lawyers and card players to make sure that they know the local rules, which can sometimes be surprisingly tricky. Even though law practice has become increasingly national in scope, we remain a nation of 52 local jurisdictions (50 states plus the District of Columbia and Puerto Rico), as well as the federal courts. Some rules, including important ones, differ from state to state, county to county, and even from courtroom to courtroom. It can be embarrassing, or worse, to run afoul of a unique state statute or idiosyncratic court rule, not to mention various unwritten practices and conventions. At best, you will be marked as an unprepared outsider. At worst, you may find yourself at a serious disadvantage, or even looking at the wrong end of a sanctions order or default judgment.

To take just one example, consider the various rules for conferring with your client during his deposition. Until not long ago, it was generally considered appropriate for a lawyer to confer with her client at just about any point during a deposition, although some courts prohibited conferences while a question was pending. Lawyers repeatedly abused this leeway, interrupting the questions and calling frequent recesses, ostensibly advising their clients, but often simply disrupting the proceeding (or worse, feeding answers to their clients).

Virtually no jurisdiction today tolerates unlimited conferring between lawyer and client, though many continue to adhere to the "no question pending" rule. Others however, have adopted far more stringent measures, prohibiting all mid-deposition conferences, save those necessary to determine whether to assert a privilege. To make matters more confusing, the reforms have been enacted through a pastiche of court rules, judicial decisions, and standing orders, meaning that there is little uniformity and sometimes no good way of finding out the local practice other than by asking around.

Similar inconsistencies abound from jurisdiction to jurisdiction on issues both mundane (tendering expert witnesses to the court) and crucial (admissibility of "prior bad acts" evidence). It is essential, therefore, to have an ironclad grasp of local procedures before you ever file an appearance or walk into a courtroom. Assume nothing.

As the following poker story illustrates, it is all too easy to get tripped up.

A tenderfoot walked into a saloon in Tombstone and sat down for a game of five-card draw. After an hour or so of indifferent success, he found himself holding four jacks. He bet the limit and was called by a grizzled old miner, while everyone else folded. Neither man took a card on the draw, and they continued raising and reraising until they hit the limit again. The miner showed his hand—two deuces, a four, a five, and a six—and reached for the pot.

"Hold on a minute, old timer," the tenderfoot yelped. "I've got four jacks."

"So you do, sonny," said the miner, "but I've got an Old Cat." He pointed to a sign on the wall, which read: An Old Cat Beats Anything.

There was no arguing with the sign, so the tenderfoot shoved over the chips and vowed to get even. Many hours later, he was delighted to see an old cat in his own hand—a pair of deuces, with a four, five, and six. Doing his best to avoid even a glimmer of a smile, he bet the limit, only to be called by the same elderly miner. Again, both men stood pat, and again they raised the limit.

The miner showed a pair of aces and reached for the pot.

"Not so fast," the tenderfoot cried. "This time I have an old cat."

"I'm sorry to hear that," said the miner, pointing to a sign on another wall: An Old Cat Is Only Good *Once* Each Night.

Court rules are seldom that arcane, but they can be almost as unpredictable and definitely just as expensive to ignore.

Anyone who has ever litigated "by the book" will be familiar with the standard advice for defending depositions: Do everything you can to limit the information given to the other side. After all, a deposition is a discovery device, used in preparation for trial. Since just about anything might be used by the opposition to bolster its case, the presumptive approach is to withhold as much as possible, within the confines of the rules. Or, as one leading handbook puts it, "There is no sense sharing information with the other side when there is no requirement of doing so."

There is a compelling logic to this approach. Information, which may eventually become evidence, is the currency of a trial. Whoever has the most information is at a substantial advantage. Consequently, a lawyer should want to find out everything the opposition knows, while keeping all of her knowledge (or as much as possible) to herself. In other words, information is viewed almost as a zero-sum commodity. And since the objective of a successful deposition is to obtain information, the objective of a successful defense must be to deny it.

To be sure, no ethical lawyer would simply disobey or flout discovery rules. But those rules are subject to considerable interpretation and are often ambiguous and flexible. Even more to the point, deposition responses depend on the particular questions asked, with no general duty to volunteer or expand. Hence, the lawyer's usual admonition is that the witness provide only the shortest possible answers, without explanation or elaboration. If opposing counsel wants more information, it's her job to ask more questions.

Most attorneys will tell you that this strategy is necessary to surprise the other side at trial. Why allow the opposition to prepare its cross-examinations, or set up impeachment, or search out other witnesses, or otherwise patch up the holes in its case?

Today, however, actual trials are few and far between, especially in civil litigation. While it is debatable whether this is good or bad from the perspective of social policy, it is an inescapable reality for lawyers. Since fewer than 3% of civil cases are tried to verdict, settlement is far and away the most common result in litigation, with as many as 30 cases settled for every trial. No competent lawyer should neglect trial preparation—if only because better preparation leads to stronger negotiating positions—but it is surely the case that depositions are most likely to be used as negotiating tools, rather than as trial bombshells.

Negotiation theory tells us that the strength of your position is a major determinant (perhaps *the* major determinant) of the outcome. The shorthand term for this concept is BATNA—best alternative to a negotiated agreement. The better your perceived BATNA, the better your negotiated result. Of course, opposing parties cannot be intimidated by your BATNA unless they know about it. Thus, a good deal of any negotiation must be devoted to a detailed description of your powerful case (without details, it would just be unpersuasive bragging). And what is it that makes your case so compelling? One factor would certainly have to be the strength of your witnesses and the quality of their expected testimony, and therefore the likelihood that you will prevail at trial.

In other words, you should usually want the other side to know about your witnesses well in advance of the trial—the better to influence their settlement posture. And what better way to educate the opposition than by showcasing your witnesses at their own depositions? Don't prepare your witnesses to give short, unrevealing answers. Encourage them to tell what they know, explaining why you represent the winning side.

Yes, this idea is hard to swallow. Lawyers have been conditioned to stash information, not give it away. And yes, the shortest-answers approach is no doubt essential with witnesses who are anxious, undependable, or ill prepared. But even those witnesses would eventually have to be prepared for direct and cross-examination if the case goes to trial. Recognizing that the deposition more or less functions as a substitute trial, it makes good sense to prepare your witnesses sooner rather than later. True, that might take slightly more time than simply drilling the witnesses to give short, correct answers, but there could be a substantial payoff in the settlement value of the case.

There may also be a serious cost to concealing even dangerous facts. If a subject is never broached in the deposition, the witness will never have a chance to rebut, explain, or accommodate the potentially damaging information. Of course, the rebuttal or explanation could always come at trial—in the exceptionally unlikely event that there is a trial. Otherwise, opposing counsel will never have to reckon with the fact that the seemingly bad facts might be neutralized or discredited by your witness's well-organized persuasive response. And the settlement will not reflect the witness's well-prepared clarity and probity.

Lawyers are creatures of habit. As a profession, we tend to respond positively to the familiar, while discounting anything novel or innovative—at least for a while. In deposition practice, lawyers have come to expect a certain level of recalcitrance from a well-prepared deponent. Indeed, a standoffish disposition is probably taken as the hallmark of a tough witness—providing as little ammunition as possible for future cross-examination.

We all know lawyers who habitually bluster about the quality of their cases, whether or not they have the actual goods to back up the bragging. In negotiation, it is important to separate bluff from strength. Thus, it is not hard to imagine that counsel's willingness to let a deponent speak might quickly be recognized as a sign of confidence. Thus, revealing information could eventually be recognized for the assertive, perhaps even aggressive, tactic that it is.

The effectiveness of intentional disclosure can be illustrated with a legendary, but true, story from the annals of professional poker. Jack "Treetop" Straus is one of the great professional poker players, winner of the 1982 World Series of Poker. His most famous play came in a round of Texas Hold'em. In this particular hand, Straus was initially dealt the worst possible hole cards—a deuce and seven of different suits (the deuce and seven are the two lowest cards that cannot be combined into a five-card straight). Ordinarily, a good player would fold such a hand, but Straus kept playing. The three-card flop consisted of a seven and two threes, giving Straus two pair (sevens and threes), but also giving everyone else a pair of threes to work with. Anyone with a big pair (higher than sevens) in the hole would beat Straus's hand. That appeared to be the case, when another player raised aggressively, indicating a very good hand. Straus nonetheless called, even though he was virtually certain that he was up against better cards (in fact, the other player was holding jacks and threes). The next up card (the turn) was a deuce. That gave Straus three pair, though it did not improve his hand, since only five cards can be used.

At that point, Straus bet $18,000, more than triple the amount of any previous bet in the game. The other player, who had been betting aggressively, suddenly paused. How could a deuce have helped Straus so much? While the other player was thinking it over, Straus leaned over the table, smiling. "I'll tell you what," he said, "You give me one of those little old $25 chips of yours, and you can see either one of my hole cards, whichever one you choose."

The other player hesitated, then tossed Straus a chip, as he pointed to one of the hole cards. Straus turned it over, revealing a deuce. The conclusion seemed obvious. Straus must have a pair of deuces in the hole (why else would he offer to show either card?), giving him a full house, deuces over threes. His opponent folded, and Straus won the pot with an inferior hand. Note that he would have achieved the same outcome if his opponent had selected the other card, a seven, since that would have indicated that Straus was holding a full house—sevens over threes.

The point of this story, in case it isn't obvious, is that Jack Straus won the hand (and became a poker legend) by voluntarily revealing information, not by concealing it. Showing his hole card was an aggressive show of strength that forced the other player out of the game.

But there was even more to the strategy than that. Good players seldom show their hole cards, so why didn't the other player recognize Straus's move as a bluff? That was due to another brilliant bit of reverse psychology. The opposing player reasoned that Straus wanted him to think he was bluffing, in order to get him to dump another $18,000 into the pot. "If Straus wants me to think he's bluffing," the loser's thinking went, "then he must really have the cards." Folding, therefore, was the only rational decision.

What good are your strengths if you keep them hidden? Or, to put it another way, good things can happen when you show your hand.

HEARTS *Ethics and Character*

Poker and law practice are both governed by rules of ethics and procedure, which are closely followed by honorable participants. The temptation to cheat is often present, especially when the stakes are high, but there is often a fine line between cheating and, shall we say, zealous self-assertion. Sketchy behavior is not always prohibited, and sometimes it is even encouraged by ambiguities in the rules. And that, of course, raises the question of character. How far are you willing to go in order to make a buck?

Consider the case of Joseph Dowd, a solo practitioner in Des Plaines, Illinois. In late 1998, he met with a woman named Mary Corcoran, whose husband had been killed in a railroad accident. Corcoran had already been offered a $1.4 million settlement, but Dowd thought the case was worth more. He advised Corcoran to retain a personal injury lawyer and eventually accompanied her to the offices of Corboy & Demetrio, one of the most prominent personal injury firms in Chicago. Following an interview with partner Thomas Demetrio, Corcoran signed a contingent fee agreement for "twenty-five per cent of any sum recovered from settlement or judgment." She also consented to a referral fee for Dowd in the amount of "forty per cent of the attorneys' fees." Referral fees are permissible in Illinois and most other states because they encourage attorneys like Dowd to send complex cases to specialists, rather than attempt to handle them alone. This referral, however, did not work out as planned.

After nearly two years of litigation, the Corboy & Demetrio lawyers came to the conclusion that they could not improve on the railroad's initial offer—so they recommended that Corcoran accept the $1.4 million offer, which had been held open by the defendant. Because they hadn't gotten an increased offer, Corboy & Demetrio voluntarily waived any fee.

Not so Joe Dowd. He insisted on payment of the referral fee—$140,000—even though he had done almost no work on the case and certainly hadn't added any value to the original offer. By his own admission, Dowd had not actively participated in the litigation on Mary Corcoran's behalf. Nonetheless, he insisted, a contract is a contract. Corboy & Demetrio were free to waive their own fee, but he was (as he testified at his deposition) a "small-town, small-time lawyer just trying to make a living," and he wanted his 140 grand.

Like every other state, Illinois has adopted an ethics rule prohibiting unreasonable attorneys' fees. Most people, including most lawyers, would no doubt agree that $140,000 is an unreasonable amount for attending a few meetings, reading a file, and making a couple of phone calls—which pretty much describes Joe Dowd's work for Mary Corcoran. Incredibly, however, the courts agreed with Dowd. The fee agreement was enforced as written; the lawyer got his money.

With one exception, the attorneys in the Corcoran case acted admirably. Corboy & Demetrio did not even ask for a fee, and another lawyer provided Mary with pro bono representation in her dispute with Dowd. Even the railroad's lawyer decently kept the $1.4 million offer on the table for more than two years. Only Joseph P. Dowd put self-enrichment ahead of every other professional value, providing plenty of ammunition for people who already think that lawyers are disgraceful parasites.

Dowd's conduct was not unethical, especially given the judicial rulings in his favor. From a lawyer's perspective, however, he surely flunked a test of character by putting his own interests ahead of his vulnerable client's. Card players, on the other hand, probably wouldn't see it that way, figuring that Dowd was just making a play for high stakes, risking his reputation and standing in the legal community in order to score a big hit. That's what gamblers call "heart." In poker, after all, greed is essential, and selfishness is a virtue.

The following lessons will explore the intricate relationship between ethics and character, in both law and poker, beginning with three types of bad behavior: lying, cheating, and scamming.

LESSON 1: *Lying*

There is a surreal nature to the gambling life, in which the ordinary rules of human interaction are suspended if not obliterated. Once the cards are fairly dealt, poker emphasizes deception, concealment, subterfuge, trickery, and outright lying. Even peeking is not prohibited if your opponent is so foolish as to flash his cards.

Anthony Holden claims that poker's elemental competition strips bare "a man's character" by revealing "makeshift metaphors for the human condition," but that is not necessarily a good thing. Some aspects of character may also be revealed by exposure to severe privation—think of starving castaways adrift in a lifeboat or pioneers stranded in a frozen mountain pass—but their desperate acts do not really tell us anything useful about hunger, much less cannibalism.

No matter what anyone says, poker requires duplicity, and therefore it can never provide a comprehensive model for life or law. Poker writer Mike Caro touts himself as the founder of the "Mike Caro University of Poker, Gaming, and Life Strategy." I have never examined the course catalog, but we can only hope that the latter part of the title is tongue in cheek. A life strategy, or law practice, based wholly on poker skills would be a disaster.

Nonetheless, some lawyers think that they can lie their way to victory, or out of a jam, or just for the sake of it. Alas, sometimes they are right. Lying lawyers are not inevitably caught; their reputations do not necessarily suffer; their friends and clients do not invariably abandon them. Often enough—indeed, too often—they are successful at bamboozling courts, winning cases, and wheedling settlements through foul means.

Contrary to the myth conveyed in some legal ethics classes, you can indeed get away with lying. But that does not make it right or acceptable. And when you are caught, the consequences can be terrible indeed, no matter how well established and powerful you may be.

On January 17, 1998, President Bill Clinton testified at what turned out to be the most significant deposition in the history of the United States. Sworn to tell the truth, he calmly lied about his affair with Monica Lewinsky, falsely stating that he was never alone with her and that he never had sexual relations with her. He would soon repeat his lies on television—"I never had sex with that woman, Ms. Lewinsky"—and several months later, he would attempt to wriggle out of the falsehoods in his videotaped grand jury testimony. But the harm was done. Clinton teetered for nearly a year on the edge of political ruin, becoming only the second president in history to be impeached.

Why did he do it? Was he trying to pull off a poker-style bluff, or was he simply the victim of hubris and poor judgment? We can never know for sure, but Clinton's autobiography gives us a glimpse of the thought processes that led to his disastrous decision (the lying, not the sex).

Paula Jones sued Clinton for an incident of sexual harassment that allegedly occurred while he was governor of Arkansas. Clinton tells us that he had an early opportunity to head off the case by paying Jones a nominal amount and helping her husband to find work in Hollywood. He refused to pay, however, "because I hadn't sexually harassed her." Instead, he hired Robert Bennett of Skadden Arps Slate Meagher & Flom to defend him.

Bennett is an exceptionally talented Washington, D.C., litigator. He eventually succeeded in getting the Jones case dismissed on summary judgment, although not until after the political damage was irreparable. There were other strategies available to Bennett that might have saved Clinton from lying under oath. Unfortunately, Clinton himself evidently foreclosed those options, insisting on a more-aggressive approach to the litigation.

Even more significantly, it appears that the president consistently lied to his own lawyer. The details have to be pieced together, but the situation seems clear.

As the fateful deposition in the Jones case approached, Clinton had every reason to know that he would be asked about his sexual relationships with female employees. As he put it:

> The presiding judge, Susan Webber Wright, had given Jones's lawyers broad permission to delve into my private life, allegedly to see if there was a pattern of sexual harassment involving any women who had held or sought state employment when I was governor or federal employment when I was president.

An astute attorney himself, Clinton was "certain that the lawyers wanted to force me to acknowledge any kind of involvement with one or more women that they could leak to the press." Moreover, he could not have doubted that Monica Lewinsky's name would come up at the deposition, because she had been disclosed on the plaintiff's witness list a month earlier.

In advance of the deposition, Clinton says he had "gone over a series of possible questions with my lawyers," concluding that "I was reasonably well prepared." He did not, however, tell them anything about Lewinsky. Did they ask him about other women? It seems impossible that they did not. Robert Bennett has honorably maintained his silence in the years since he represented Clinton, but no competent lawyer would have failed to ask a client about every person named on the opposing side's witness list. Given the transparency of the plaintiff's tactics—trying to force Clinton to talk about sexual liaisons—we can be virtually certain that Bennett put the question directly to the president.

Stating it bluntly, then, Clinton always expected to be asked about Lewinsky, and he always planned to lie, keeping his lawyer in the dark so that he could be sure to get away with it.

True to form, Jones's lawyers used the deposition to dig into Clinton's relationship with Lewinsky. As Clinton recalls, they asked "how well I knew her, whether we had ever exchanged gifts, whether we had ever talked on the phone, and if I had had 'sexual relations' with her." Silently relying on Judge Wright's somewhat incomplete definition, Clinton "answered no to the 'sexual relations' question."

During a break in the testimony, Clinton lied to his lawyers again about Lewinsky. "My legal team was perplexed," he says, "because Lewinsky's name had shown up on the plaintiff's list of potential witnesses only in early December, and she had been given a subpoena to appear as a witness two weeks later." Of course, they were only perplexed because Clinton refused to tell the truth. Instead, he continued to dissemble: "I didn't tell them about my relationship with her, but I did say I was unsure of exactly what the curious definition of sexual relations meant."

Can we really believe that the president hinted so broadly to his lawyers that a less "curious" definition would lead to a more-explicit answer? Again, we will probably never learn Bennett's version, but surely he would have put two and two together. Imagine how the conversation might have gone between lawyer and client (based solely on Clinton's own account):

BENNETT: Mr. President, we are perplexed. Why are
they asking you about sexual relations with Monica Lewinsky?

CLINTON: I don't know. But I am unsure what is
meant by the curious definition of "sexual relations."

Is it even remotely conceivable that Bennett would have
failed to ask a single follow-up question? Of course not. So
we are left with only two plausible scenarios. Either Clinton's
memoir is, shall we say, rather inaccurate about the hint to
Bennett (diverting some of the blame to his lawyer for not
figuring out what was going on), or Bennett actually pur-
sued the hint but obtained only more misinformation from
his client.

Nearly all of Clinton's woes, up to and including his
impeachment, are traceable to his perjury in the Jones deposition. Ultimately, there was no proof that he ever induced
anyone else to lie, nor that he concealed evidence, nor that he
destroyed gifts from Monica Lewinsky. But there can be no
doubt (among any but the most credulous) that he flatly lied
in his deposition and was later loquaciously evasive about it
when he testified before a grand jury. Clinton, alas, remains
in denial. He wasn't lying, he writes; it was merely that he
"had not been trying to be helpful to the Jones lawyers." Or,
as he testified to the grand jury, "I was determined to walk
through the minefield of this deposition without violating
the law, and I believe I did."

As we all know, he was badly mistaken. Ken Starr and
the House of Representatives' impeachment managers obviously concluded that Clinton had violated the law—although
that was not exactly an objective assessment. But so too did

Ethics and Character

Judge Susan Webber Wright, who held Clinton in contempt of court for his false testimony. And Clinton was also compelled to surrender his Arkansas law license because his "evasive and misleading answers" were "prejudicial to the administration of justice."

That behavior would have been fine at a poker table where, according to Mike Caro, "it's perfectly permissible to lie about your hands and about the way you play them. In fact, it's part of the psychology of winning. And once in a while, you should throw in the truth, just to keep opponents off balance." But that just tells us that poker cannot provide useful guidance for life, law, or politics.

In that regard, Andy Bellin candidly admits that poker has ruined nearly "every relationship I've ever had in my life" because "coming home at four in the morning smelling of booze and cigarettes, with a couple of thousand dollars less in my pocket than I left the house with, just ain't good for a relationship." He goes on in that vein for pages, debunking the romantic myths of the gambling life. The writer Michael Konik says the same thing more bluntly: "In poker you have to lie to win; in life telling lies will only make you lose."

And as Bill Clinton learned to the nation's dismay, telling lies in legal proceedings can get you disbarred.

LESSON 2: *Cheating*

Poker has always been plagued by cheaters; some historians even suggest that it was invented by swindlers, with the above-board game simply serving as a cover for various forms of unseen chicanery. But even if poker's origin was not quite so devious, it is true—either ironically or unremarkably—that the first published account of a poker game involved cheating on a Mississippi riverboat. In 1844, an itinerant British actor named Joseph Cowell published his memoirs, including the story of a December 1829 riverboat trip from Louisville to New Orleans. On one "foggy, wretched night," as the passengers entertained themselves by playing cards in the main cabin, the steamboat ran aground, causing "a most tremendous concussion, as if all-powerful nature had shut his hand upon us." All of the passengers ran to the exits, fearful that the boiler had exploded,

> with the exception of one of the poker players: a gentleman in green spectacles, a gold guard-chain, long and thick enough to moor a dog, and a brilliant diamond breast pin; he was, apparently, quietly shuffling and cutting the poker pack for his own amusement.

Of course, the gentleman—dressed as he was in antebellum bling-bling—was a card sharp, or black-leg, as they were called in those days. And far from shuffling the cards for his own amusement, he was rearranging the deck to his own advantage. Unfortunately for him, he was apparently distracted by the commotion, and he accidentally gave the winning cards to another player. Here is how the hand played out, after everyone returned to the table:

> It was his turn to deal, and when he ended, he did not lift his cards, but sat watching quietly the countenances of the others. The man on his left had bet ten dollars; a young lawyer . . . bet ten more; at the time, fortunately for him, he was unconscious of the real value of his hand, and consequently did not betray by his manner, as greenhorns mostly do, his certainty of winning.

Ethics and Character

The next player called the first two bets and raised $500.

"I must see that," said Green Spectacles, who now took up his hand with "I am sure to win," trembling at his fingers' ends; for you couldn't see his eyes through his glasses; he paused a moment in disappointed astonishment, and sighed, "I pass," and threw his cards upon the table.

The following player called the $500 and raised "one thousand dollars better."

The young lawyer, who had had time to calculate the power of his hand—four kings with an ace—it could not be beat! But still he hesitated at the impossibility; as if he thought it could—looked at the money staked and then at his hand again, and, lingeringly, put his wallet on the table and called.

The other players also called the bet, as well they should have. One of them held four queens and an ace, and the other had four jacks with an ace. It was a deal designed to prompt maximum betting, and only the lawyer's naiveté prevented the pot from growing even bigger. Even still, he was "agreeably astonished" to pocket more than $2,000 as a result of his amazing good luck. But of course, it had not been luck at all. The dealer had intended the four kings for himself, planning to give the young lawyer four tens, along with the final ace.

The truth was, the cards had been *put up* or *stacked*, as it is called, by the guard-chain-man . . . but the excitement of the time had caused him to make a slight mistake in the distribution of the hand. He was one of many who followed card playing for a living but not properly coming under the denomination of gentleman sportsman, who alone depends on his superior skill. But in that pursuit, as in all others, even among the players, some black-sheep and black-legs will creep in, as in the present instance.

It bears noting, at least for present purposes, that it was a young lawyer who won the hand with honest play and in fact refrained from exploiting his advantage. He was a credit to our profession, if not to the early entrepreneurs of poker.

Through the years, poker devotees have delighted in the stories of rogues and tricksters, inspiring W. C. Fields's famous quotation that "a thing worth having is a thing worth cheating for," as well as Walter Matthau's more nuanced observation that poker "exemplifies the worst aspects of capitalism that have made our country so great." No one exactly condones cheating in the present tense, but almost everyone gets a kick out of the exploits of daring old-timers.

The great problem, of course, is that cheating can work, especially when there are amateurs at the table. Attracted by large amounts of easy money—in a game where, by definition, everyone is trying to get something for nothing—cheaters have developed a broad array of schemes and devices to assure that they win. At the lowest level, cheating might involve nothing more than "shorting the pot," or throwing in fewer chips than called for. Over the course of many hours, that can save you a significant amount on losing hands without affecting the take when you win.

A more-sophisticated cheater will bring a marked deck into the game, giving him the great advantage of reading everyone else's hands. He won't win more than his share of pots, but he will know when to fold and he will recognize everyone's bluffs, allowing him to maximize his profits and minimize his losses. For just that reason, however, it is extremely difficult to smuggle a dirty deck into a serious poker game; everyone will insist on using sealed decks that are frequently changed. Moreover, marked cards provide physical evidence of cheating, making it possible to lay blame and extract retribution when a malefactor is caught.

At the top of the cheaters' hierarchy are the card manipulators, or "deck mechanics," who use sleight-of-hand techniques to stack the deck, fake shuffles and cuts, or deal "seconds." The great advantage of card manipulation is that it leaves no evidence once the hand is dealt. It would be suspicious, of course, bordering on proof, if you always won on your own deal, so mechanics often work with partners, arriving and leaving separately but dealing each other winning hands at seemingly safe intervals. Because they rely on skill and countless hours of practice, deck mechanics often consider themselves to be artists rather than crooks, although that is nothing more than a transparent rationalization.

Then again, some amount of rationalization is probably essential to cheating (except among the most amoral sociopaths), and it can sometimes lead to complex questions of metaphysics. In his youth, when he was still working as Monty's understudy, Herbert Yardley spotted a cheater at the table, an out-of-towner named Lolly Horne, who was dealing himself winning cards. Yardley reported his suspicions to his boss, who watched the next deal and then pulled the stranger into the back room.

"Where'd you learn to deal seconds?" Monty demanded.

"I don't know what you mean."

"You can tell me about it or I'll break both those beautiful goddamned hands of yours," Monty threatened.

"All right," Lolly replied in an even voice, showing resignation but no fear. "I was dealing seconds. How did you know?"

"They make a slight swish when you pull them from the deck, as you damn well know," said Monty. "Don't you ever feel sorry for the suckers you fleece?"

"No, I don't," answered Lolly, seizing an opportunity for self-justification. "My method is painless. I give them the ax. You bleed them to death slowly."

"Curious philosophy for a card sharp," replied Monty, reacting to the accusation. "At least the players get a square gamble here."

"Between themselves they do," insisted Lolly, "not with you playing. You won't play unless you think you have the best hand. I won't play unless I know I have the best hand, unless I deliberately want another to win. Will you play with a weak hand?"

"Hell no!"

"Will a sucker?"

"The sucker doesn't know what a good hand is. That's the reason he's a sucker."

"Monty," the unrepentant cheater explained, "it's an old matter of debate. You win on superior expertise and finesse; I win because I am a card manipulator. You study percentages; I deal seconds. Essentially we are no different. In the end we both bleed the sucker."

Monty had no real answer, or at least none that Yardley saw fit to report. His whole approach to the game was to minimize the element of chance by betting only on highly favorable odds and making it nearly impossible to lose.

Ethics and Character

Lolly merely went one step further, removing luck entirely by manipulating the cards. Either way, the suckers had no chance.

Yardley recognized as much in one of his later colloquies with Monty. "It looks like poker, as you play it, is a sort of legalized theft."

"Yes it is," Monty admitted, "and only once removed from playing like a card sharp."

Now, there is a distinction that lawyers can appreciate, even if deck mechanics do not. Monty's approach was *legalized* theft—the adjective makes all the difference—meaning that he played strictly within the agreed-upon rules. Sure, he took advantage of the simpletons, but he did it with their consent. Everyone at the table had equal knowledge of the rules and equal opportunity to play as tightly as Monty. They foolishly chose not to, or knowing that they couldn't play that way, they foolishly chose to continue anyhow. The crucial difference in Lolly's case is that no one ever consents to a stacked deck. Monty could have shared his secret with everyone at the table—"When I play, I either think I have the best hand or the makings of one"—and he still would have won. If Lolly had shared his secret, no one would have played with him.

LESSON 3: *Scamming*

The golden age of poker scamming is mostly in the past. With the spread of casino gambling beyond Nevada and New Jersey, the legalization of card rooms in California, and the existence in many big cities of illegal-but-tolerated card clubs, professional dealers have eliminated many opportunities for deck mechanics and other sharps to ply their dodgy trade. Yes, there are still hustlers who try to exploit friendly games with shifty scams and foul tactics, but they are probably a dying breed, pushed even closer to extinction by the growing popularity of tournament and Internet poker. It is relatively easy, therefore, to look back on the good old days when rogues and scoundrels roamed from state to state, fleecing suckers and making reputations. Like other forms of outlawry, cheating can seem romantic—so long as it happened to someone else.

In law, we have the opposite phenomenon. We look back to a different sort of golden age, populated by men (and a few women) of steely integrity, who were more concerned with principles than with winning at any cost. While poker has become more respectable and mainstream, law practice has degenerated—so the story line goes—until it is now the domain of hucksters, cads, deceivers, spoliators, fabricators, and various other betrayers of civility. Well, law practice has certainly changed over the decades, in some ways for the worse, but it is not as bad as all that. Most lawyers, no matter how aggressive or even offensive, still try to play by the rules. Perhaps they exploit every technicality, but they still care about the technicalities and do not intentionally go beyond them.

At some point, therefore, in both law and poker, cheating becomes a technical question. What do the rules allow, and what do they prohibit? The answers are usually quite clear, but sometimes—especially in a gray area that might be called "scamming"—they can be surprisingly subtle.

The poker film *A Big Hand for the Little Lady* (1966) engagingly explores the scammy intersection of law and ethics, though perhaps not as the director intended. Set in the late nineteenth century, the story opens when five of the wealthi-est men in the unnamed "Territory" gather at a hotel-cum-saloon for their annual high-stakes poker game. As fate would have it, a pioneer family finds itself stuck in town, due to a broken wagon wheel, and forced to stay at the same hotel. The wimpy father, named Meredith (played by Henry Fonda), is a recovering poker addict, who becomes transfixed by the idea of the big game. He implores his stern wife, Mary (played by Joanne Woodward), to let him watch the game while she takes their wagon to the blacksmith's. She relents after much begging, but only if he promises not to play and only if he brings along their 12-year-old son as a witness.

Needless to say, Meredith soon wheedles his way into the game, despite his son's protests, and quickly loses most of his $1,000 stake. Then, with only a handful of chips remaining, he is seemingly dealt a monster hand. He bets everything he has on the table, only to be raised and reraised by the other players, every one of whom apparently has monster cards of his own. Out of chips, Meredith cannot call the raises, and the others, smelling blood in the water, remind him that they are playing by "western rules." If you can't call, you lose, no matter how good your cards. Desperate and panicked, Meredith races up to his room and tears apart the family's bags, searching for their hidden nest egg. Back at the table, he wagers the entire $4,000, only to be raised again, and put back in the same western-rules predicament. Suddenly, as he is twisting in despair, he suffers a heart attack and must be taken to the next room to be cared for by the local doctor. Fortunately, he has the presence of mind to place his cards face down on the table just as he collapses.

Mary arrives moments later, frantic about the health of her husband. Reassured by Doc Scully (Burgess Meredith) that nothing more can be done for her husband, she enters the card room, only to learn of the family's impending financial disaster. With no alternative, she announces that she will play out her husband's hand. "What happens next?" she asks the gentlemen at the table, exposing her complete ignorance of poker. Alas, they explain to her, the bet has been raised, and she must either call or lose everything.

"Is there a bank in this town?" she asks.

Yes, there is one across the street, they tell her. But what good will that do?

She will borrow the money, she tells them, using her poker hand as collateral. They all have a good laugh at the idea. Who ever heard of borrowing money for a poker hand, and besides, the local banker is known to hate gambling.

Nonetheless, Mary, cards in hand, marches everyone across the street to the bank. They must accompany her to keep the game honest, lest she surreptitiously replace her cards. And no one can stay behind for the same reason, lest they monkey with their own hands.

Banker Ballinger (played by Paul Ford) is skeptical, as predicted. He has never heard of such an outlandish idea. How could any of the gentlemen even be party to such an outrage? Then Mary shows him her cards. His eyes open wide, then wider, as he barely suppresses a gasp. He has never seen such a hand. He immediately opens the safe and pulls out a stack of bills, simultaneously making a deal with Mary to split the pot with interest. They march back to the card room, where the banker makes a huge raise. Everyone else folds, of course, realizing that a coldhearted number-cruncher like Ballinger would never bet that much money on anything less than a sure thing. Mary saves the farm, Meredith apparently recovers, and the day is saved.

Ethics and Character

But it was all a scam. Mary and Meredith are actually professional card sharps (and not married), as is their "son," who is a Huck Finn–type juvenile adventurer. Doc Scully was in on the deal, as was banker Ballinger who, in fact, orchestrated the whole thing in retribution for a long-ago land swindle.

Cheerfully dividing the swag, Ballinger cautions his confederates to avoid returning to town or else the beaten players will "figure out that we cheated them."

"We did not cheat them," replies Mary indignantly, "we bluffed them. That's the nature of the game." And everyone smiles.

It is a happy ending, but it does not exactly answer the deep question. Was it cheating, or was it bluffing? There was certainly plenty of deception. Meredith faked a heart attack, Doc faked a diagnosis, Mary faked ignorance of poker, and Ballinger faked surprise at the fake strength of her hand. Everyone on the winning side was lying in clever and novel ways.

On the other hand, the money was real. Ballinger was not faking when he pulled thousands of dollars out of his safe, bought into the game, and pushed his chips into the pot. Any one of the other five players could have called the bluff— we know they all had good cards, because they were all betting like crazy until Ballinger showed up—and won the hand. Having attempted to intimidate Meredith, via the western rules, into losing his entire stake, they were now intimidated themselves by Ballinger's aggressive wager.

"The art of the bluff always involves an element of acting," according to A. Alvarez, so the real question is whether Ballinger and company went too far. What, if anything, did the western rules have to say about bald-faced lying?

As in law school classes, we can get at least part of the answer by slightly changing the hypothetical. What if Ballinger, when he laid his chips on the table, had told the others that he might be lying. "You know," he might have said, "these cards may not really be so impressive. This could all be part of an elaborate bluff." We can be virtually certain that they would have folded anyhow, figuring that he was only trying to inveigle them into the pot. By that standard, as we saw in the previous section regarding Monty's style, the play was within the rules.

But there are still two problems. Today, any sort of teamwork is considered cheating, though we don't know how the western rules handled clandestine confederates. We also don't know what would have happened if Ballinger had said something like, "Gentlemen, you should consider the possibility that the little lady and I might be in cahoots." Perhaps they would have folded in any event. Nonetheless, it is hard to believe that anyone would willingly play in a game that included elaborately staged scenarios with the undisclosed participation of outsiders.

There is a reasonably similar anecdote in the annals of lawyers' dirty tricks. The story is told of a wily insurance company lawyer, defending a heart-wrenching wrongful death case. The plaintiff was a middle-aged gentleman, whose wife of 30 years had been run over by the defendant's truck. Liability was pretty certain, but the damages were far from clear. The poor woman had died instantly, so there could be little compensation for her pain and suffering. She had not been employed outside the home, so neither were there lost wages. The bulk of the damages, therefore, would have to be for loss of consortium and companionship. With decades yet to live, the plaintiff faced a lonely life as a bereft widower. Such was the case that the plaintiff presented to the jury—the story of a faithful and dedicated couple, now separated forever.

Realizing that cross-examination would be fruitless, if not self-defeating, and lacking any evidence of his own, the defense lawyer seized upon a plan. He located an attractive young actress and paid her to sit in the courtroom audience, dressed fashionably and slightly provocatively (not too much, of course). At every recess, she was instructed to catch the plaintiff's eye, waving to him or possibly sidling over to him. At least once, she managed to kiss his cheek.

No one knew who she was, much less that she was employed by the defense counsel, but the message to the jury was clear. The plaintiff had found someone new, and any damage award was likely to be spent on her. It is said that the outraged jury gave him peanuts.

The story may well be apocryphal, or at least exaggerated, but it has proven useful as a legal ethics teaching tool. The defense lawyer obviously created the false—but no less effective—impression that the plaintiff was not appropriately mourning his wife. But was it unethical? He made no untrue statements, introduced no phony evidence, and he did not even refer to the young woman during his final argument. He simply allowed the jurors to draw their own conclusions (without, by the way, so much as an objection from plaintiff's counsel).

Sure, it seems rotten to plant an actress in the audience, but what exactly is wrong with it?

Law students frequently have difficulty articulating their objections, but practicing lawyers usually get right to the heart of it. The defense lawyer, cagey as he was, used a subterfuge to bring inadmissible matter before the jury. He had, in fact, created false evidence even though he did not formally offer it in evidence. Indeed, the wrong was compounded by its nonrecord nature, because that deprived the plaintiff of an opportunity to object. A specific rule covers this situation, which provides that a lawyer may not "allude to any matter that the lawyer does not reasonably believe is relevant or that will not be supported by admissible evidence." Counsel "alluded" to the bogus relationship between the actress and the plaintiff when he planted her in the jury's presence and instructed her to exhibit contrived signs of affection.

As lawyers and card players, then, we implicitly consent to the feints and ploys of our opponents, but only if they are straightforward about their identities. They have to tell us who is truly in the game and who is not. No ringers allowed.

LESSON 4: *Banking the Proceeds*

In the summer of 2001, a curious law student posted a question on an Internet gambling forum, wondering whether lawyers tend to be good poker players. The inquiry prompted a long discussion thread, including this response: "I think lawyers, especially patent attorneys from southeastern Connecticut, are about the best poker players in the world." The writer was talking about himself, of course, but it was not an idle boast. Greg "Fossilman" Raymer, then working as patent counsel for a large pharmaceutical firm, went on to win the 2004 World Series of Poker championship.

Born in North Dakota, Raymer began playing nickel-and-dime poker during college and then went to law school at the University of Minnesota, where he also earned a master's degree in biochemistry. He began to study poker seriously while working at a big intellectual-property law firm in Chicago and continued playing as he moved to Milwaukee and San Diego before settling in Connecticut. Eventually, he began playing poker in tournaments and on the Internet, becoming a consistent winner.

Following his victory at the WSOP, Raymer attributed much of his success to his ability to pay attention to detail, a talent that he no doubt honed during his years as a patent lawyer. "Maybe I pay more attention than other people," he explained to an interviewer. "I don't go on tilt too easily. I take short stack factors into account, recognizing that people can make desperation calls without even looking at their cards and be big favorites. It sounds obvious, but a lot of people ignore that one." Proud of his ability to calculate the right bet size, he criticized players who go all in too often.

Raymer's best moves at the WSOP came on the last day, when he noticed that many of his opponents were becoming risk averse. "A lot of decisions in poker are very marginal," he said. At critical moments, many players tend to tip their decisions toward the safe side, by folding. "I sized up who was playing it safe and took advantage of that . . . by pushing people around and stealing blinds and antes." Litigation by other means.

Raymer entered the WSOP hoping to win enough money to quit his job and open a solo practice. Instead, the championship brought him more than $5 million. He is now a full-time card player who describes himself as a "former patent lawyer."

There are many other stories about lawyers who have used their poker skills to change careers, although not always with such happy endings. Richard Nixon, a graduate of the Duke University Law School, was a formidable poker player, having learned the game in the navy. One of his ship-mates described him as among the best he had ever seen. "He played a quiet game, but wasn't afraid of taking chances. He wasn't afraid of running a bluff. Sometimes the stakes were pretty big, but Nick had daring and a flair for knowing what to do."

Nixon was so successful at the card table that he used his winnings to finance his first campaign for the U.S. House of Representatives. That unique form of campaign funding caused some controversy, especially as Nixon's political career progressed, but one of his former profes-sors put it into perspective: "A man who couldn't hold a hand in a first-class poker game is not fit to be President of the United States."

Perhaps so, but Nixon's penchant for bluffing would later cause his downfall. When the Watergate burglary was discovered and eventually tied to the White House, Nixon's first reaction was to engineer a massive cover-up. Even as the plot unraveled, Nixon continued to stonewall the inves-tigation, which culminated in his firing of special prosecu-tor Archibald Cox in the infamous Saturday night massacre. That was a huge provocation that dramatically raised the stakes. There were immediate calls for his impeachment, but Nixon was convinced that Congress would never call his bet, and he put the full weight of his office behind one of the greatest bluffs in history.

David Spanier observed that Nixon's bluff was not entirely misconceived:

> After all, the White House had the immense advan-tage of running the game, so to speak, and of exer-cising its control over the principal players. The bluff

Ethics and Character

failed in the end because *the hands were recorded* in the form of the tapes. That was why the cover-up was ultimately exposed. If the tapes had been destroyed instead of being doctored, the probability is that Congress would not have nerved itself to bring in a Bill of Impeachment, and Richard Nixon's greatest bluff would have "held."

Nixon, as we know today, was holding a badly busted hand. Far from an ace in the hole, his pocket cards only made things worse. Nonetheless, he thought that he could show enough strength to bet the presidency, assuming that Congress would eventually fold. What he didn't count on, of course, was the Supreme Court's unanimous ruling in *United States v. Nixon,* forcing him to disclose his secret tapes—including the mysterious and never-explained 18-minute gap—to the Watergate investigators. Left with nothing more to bet, the bluff crumbled. Nixon became the only president in U.S. history to resign from office, with no one to blame but himself.

LESSON 5: *The Right Stuff*

Poker has always been popular among political figures. George Washington kept a careful account of his successes and failures at cards, and many modern presidents—including Harry Truman, Dwight Eisenhower, and Richard Nixon—have been poker players. Part of the attraction must surely be the permissibility of deception, as important in politics, alas, as it is in poker. Another part of the attraction must be the opportunity to practice bluffing, also a crucial political skill.

A story is often told about a poker game between Daniel Webster (1782–1852) and Henry Clay (1777–1852), two of the most important American political leaders in the years before the Civil War. Both men were elected many times to both the House and the Senate, each served as secretary of state, and both were prominent lawyers, though Webster was far more successful (he argued and won *McCulloch v. Maryland* in the Supreme Court). Contemporaries for years in Washington, D.C., and colleagues in the Whig party, they may have played cards together many times, although only one extraordinary hand of five-card draw is remembered today. Here is how David Spanier related it in his book *Total Poker*:

> With Webster dealing, Clay drew one card on the draw and Webster stood pat. The two went on raising each other until each had $2000 on the table. At this stage Clay stopped reraising and called. According to this account Webster laughed sheepishly and threw down his cards. "I only have a pair of deuces," he said. Clay laughed too. "The pot is yours," he said. "I only have an ace high."

The usual point of the story is that both men were bluffing at high stakes ($2,000 was a small fortune in the early nineteenth century), giving us some insight into their characters. Alvarez, impressed by their aggressiveness, observes that "Clay and Webster were hard, ambitious men as well as fearless gamblers, and when they faced each other head-to-head their pride was on the line. Each smelled the other's weakness and was determined not to blink."

Ethics and Character

But there is a more significant moral than that. It should be obvious that Henry Clay misplayed his hand. Having set out to bluff, when holding virtually nothing, it was a clear mistake for him to call Webster's last bet. Rather, he should either have continued the bluff (by raising) or cut his losses (by folding). By calling instead, he only ensured his loss while throwing an unnecessary bet into the pot.

It was Webster who played the hand correctly, raising until the end and successfully wearing down his opponent. Yes, he stood a good chance of losing—the odds were heavy that Clay could beat a pair of deuces—but even then his bets could have paid off on future hands. After all, Webster demonstrated that he had the nerve to back his play to the end, while Clay showed that he could be pushed into making a bad decision. Both men would surely remember that as the game continued—and probably in Congress and the courtroom as well.

But does the story really tell us anything about either man's capabilities as a politician? Webster aspired dearly to the presidency, but he managed to run only once, losing badly in 1836. Clay, however, did even worse. He ran for the presidency three times, becoming the only man ever to lead three different parties to defeat. Most telling was the election of 1824, which was thrown into the House of Representatives when none of the four major candidates received a majority of the electoral vote. Clay gave his support to John Quincy Adams in exchange for appointment as secretary of state. That agreement was immediately denounced as a "corrupt bargain" by the supporters of Andrew Jackson, who was the winner of the popular vote. The damage to Clay's reputation was substantial and enduring, perhaps crippling his two subsequent presidential campaigns.

In his lifetime, Clay was nicknamed "The Great Compromiser," more famous for brokering deals than for adhering to a set of principles. To this day, many historians believe that the corrupt bargain, as it has been known ever since, was evidence that Clay ultimately lacked the courage of his convictions. Be that as it may, he certainly lacked the courage to carry through on his bluffs.

LESSON 6: *Moral Hazards*

Like Richard Nixon, who grew reflective in his later years, most card players recognize that they must accept the consequences of their own bluffs and losses. Lawyers, however, also have to worry about their clients, which raises a problem that philosophers call a "moral hazard."

In poker, there is a "right play" for every situation, based on the concepts of expected value and pot odds. The right play optimizes your total return, even if it fails to produce profits in a given situation, because the odds imply that eventual gains will outweigh losses. In other words, you can win by losing, so long as you keep playing. Given the right rate of return, you can take nine chances on a ten-to-one shot, for example, because one of the bets will ultimately pay off handsomely.

This works because poker success is measured in the long run, not in a single game and certainly not on the basis of a single hand. Daily performance is inconsequential. Instead, professional poker players view their careers as a single, unending game, in which they are either ahead or behind. As one championship player explained to Alvarez:

Ethics and Character

I mean, how long is a poker game? If you play for a living, there is no end to it. Just because it breaks up doesn't mean it ends. The players go away, but they are still thinking about it. . . . And they'll be there again the next day. Them or someone else.

Poker players can take the long view, absorbing losses in the name of expected value, because they play with their own money. The long run for them is continuous because the profits and losses are all from the same pocket.

Lawyers, on the other hand, have clients, most of whom are not repeat players. Clients' interests, therefore, are generally episodic rather than continuous. The client wants to win the current case and doesn't care if your exquisitely calculated tactic will succeed fabulously for some other litigant down the road. Therefore, clients tend to care only about immediate returns, rather than expected value.

This situation creates a classic moral hazard, meaning that the decision maker has an incentive to take unnecessary risks because she will not bear the cost of her own choices. Moral hazards are familiar in economic life, especially when insurance is available. People imprudently rebuild their homes on flood plains, for example, because federal insurance programs will reimburse them when the inevitable disaster strikes. More commonly, medical patients are often willing and eager to undergo borderline treatments, and physicians are willing to administer them, because an insurance company or other third-party payer will cover the expense.

When one party gets the expected benefit, while another accepts the certain cost, you are looking at a moral hazard. While this is unavoidable, at least to some degree, in the business world, insurance companies and large corporations can cope with the inherent problem through cost spreading and diversification. Lawyers' clients, however, typically have no such means at their disposal. Instead, they depend on their lawyers' sense of professionalism and commitment to their fiduciary duty.

Still, there can be great temptation in law practice to risk one client's welfare for the sake of another. In its most crass form, such behavior is strictly forbidden by the *Model Rules of Professional Conduct*, which prohibit making an "aggregate settlement of claims" unless each client consents after full disclosure. Most lawyers instinctively realize that a two-for-one deal can betray an unwary client (you cannot use one case as a "sweetener" when settling another), but less-blatant situations can be harder to recognize.

It would be wrong, for example, for a criminal defense lawyer to encourage a client to plead guilty simply for fear of annoying the local prosecutor. And it would be wrong for any lawyer, civil or criminal, to refrain from making a valid recusal motion for fear of offending the judge. There could be a palpable benefit to the lawyer, and his future clients, in each situation—a potentially cooperative prosecutor when it comes to later plea bargains and a nonresentful judge in subsequent cases—but it would be the current client who bears the cost of the decision, so the trade-off is not permissible. Instead, the decision must be made for the sole benefit of the current client, based on the lawyer's independent judgment. Plead guilty or go to trial, as the client's interests dictate and not to curry favor with the prosecutor. And if a client's case requires a recusal motion, well, so be it, even if the judge might be annoyed at you for weeks or months to come.

This is not to say that the concept of expected value is useless to lawyers. High-volume personal-injury lawyers, for example, are known to accept dozens of relatively marginal cases on the theory that a small fraction of them will pan out. This is a fairly close analogue to the poker player's concept of positive expectation. Note, however, that in accepting a case the lawyer is acting on his own behalf, thus there is no moral hazard. Once a case has been accepted, the lawyer must handle it advantageously to the client without regard to the needs or goals of others.

Successful poker players always take the long view, but lawyers must assess positive expectations on a shorter time frame, in the context of a single case. As an agent, the lawyer must doggedly pursue his client's best interests, being careful not to sacrifice them for his own advantage or the gain of another. This requires lawyers to be far more conservative than poker players when it comes to banking on the odds.

LESSON 7: *Self-Control*

One of the most important lessons in poker is that you must not attempt to win every pot. Playing too many hands is the surest way to lose money, even if it seems like fun at the time. Loose play is always enticing, because it creates more action, but self-restraint is by far the better strategy. Only by abandoning the goal of short-term victories can you begin to concentrate on long-term profits.

No doubt, that is easier said than done. Mike Caro has come up with a mantra that can help you to resist temptation. "You don't get paid to win pots," he says, "you get paid to make the right decisions." Folding at the right time can be the best possible decision, because it saves money that you would otherwise lose. Correctly reading another player's slow play or check-raise can save even more money, and distinguishing bluffs from the nuts might be the most important skill of all. Quality decisions can and do win, of course, but more often they will keep you from playing losing hands.

It would be easy to become "the grand champion of winning pots," as Caro puts it, because you would only need to bet most hands all the way to the river. That way, you would win on your premium hands, and you would also hit every possible long shot. You would end up winning more pots than anyone else, but you would also multiply your losses by several orders of magnitude. There has never been a statistical study, but it is likely that the players who win the most pots are the first ones to go broke.

For lawyers, the virtue of self-control may be even more important, especially when it comes to cross-examination. You do not get paid to trounce witnesses, as Caro might say, you get paid to make the right decisions. And the right decision, in the context of an entire case, might very well be to take it easy on a witness or even to forgo cross-examination altogether.

Glen Kanwit, a litigator with a large national law firm, learned the hard way about the perils of trying to win all the time. Many years ago, he was defending a company in an unfair product-of-origin labeling case. "My client," says Kanwit, "imported every component in an electrical device, assembled it in New Jersey, and labeled the retail product 'Made in the USA.' . . . I was not very happy about defending that position in front of a jury, but that was the party paying for my services."

The plaintiff's chief executive officer was a grandfatherly type—genial but not very bright—whose testimony was central to the opposing case. He more or less bumbled through his direct examination but managed to make several important points. Kanwit thought he saw an opening and launched a withering cross-examination, "complete with stylish impeachments" from the gentleman's deposition. Kanwit sat down, satisfied that he had won the encounter—as indeed he had, in lawyering terms.

The case settled later in the trial, so it never went to verdict. Kanwit did have an opportunity to interview the jurors, however, and he was stunned by their reactions. "They did not like my client very much in the first place," he says, "but they absolutely hated him after that marvelous cross examination. They all loved the humble grandfather, and felt sorry for him in the wake of my devastating onslaught."

"A trial is not performance art," reflects Kanwit today. "It is about persuasion, which can take a different form in different situations." As an antidote to overzealousness and an incentive to self-control, he suggests watching a few scenes from the comedy *My Cousin Vinnie* (1992).

The film opens as Bill Gambini (Ralph Macchio) and Stan Rothenstein (Mitchell Whitfield), best friends from New York, are driving through Alabama on their way to Los Angeles to attend film school. Disaster strikes when they are mistakenly identified as the killers of a convenience-store clerk and charged with murder in Beechum County. Lacking funds and resources, they persuade Bill's cousin Vinnie Gambini (the incomparable Joe Pesci) to head south and defend them.

Vincent Gambini, admitted to the bar only six weeks earlier (having flunked five times before he passed the exam) is a classic Brooklyn wiseacre. He is positive that he can win the case, despite his lack of experience, complete unfamiliarity with local practice, and the palpable hostility of Judge

Chamberlain Haller (Fred Gwynne, in the last performance
of his life). Still, assisted by his beautiful and equally wise-
cracking fiancée, Mona Lisa Vito (Marisa Tomei), he proves
his natural talent in the courtroom—including his ability to
quickly change gears.

The first witness for the prosecution is the slovenly Sam
Tipton, a good old boy who is obviously eager to help the
prosecution. Tipton testifies that he saw the defendants
enter the convenience store—the Sac-O-Suds—while he was
making his breakfast. Then he heard a gunshot and saw
them run out and drive off in their green convertible. After
identifying both defendants and a photo of their car, Tipton
is tendered for cross-examination. It quickly becomes apparent that the streetwise Vinnie is not about to take any crap
from this witness:

"Would you say you got a better look at them goin' in,
and not so much goin' out?" he asks.

"You could say that," answers Tipton.

"I did say that," retorts Vinnie, "would you say that?"

"Yeah."

"So is it possible that the two defendants entered the
store, then left, then two different men drive up in a similar
looking car, go in, shoot the clerk and then leave?"

"No, they didn't have enough time," says Tipton defi-
antly.

"Well, how much time was they in the store?"

"Five minutes."

"Did you look at your watch?" asks Vinnie, setting up
the kill.

"No."

"Oh, I remember. You testified earlier that the boys went
into the store, and you had just begun to make breakfast.

You were just waiting to eat and you heard a gunshot. So obviously it takes you five minutes to make breakfast."

"That's right," answers Tipton, taking the bait.

"Do you remember what you had?"

"Eggs and grits."

"Instant grits?"

"No self-respecting southerner uses instant grits," scoffs the witness. "I take pride in my grits."

"Well," asks Vinnie, "how could it take you 5 minutes to cook your grits when it takes the entire great eating world 20 minutes?"

"I dunno," says Tipton, looking for a way out. "I'm a fast cook, I guess."

"Did you say you're a fast cook? That's it?" asks Vinnie, as sarcasm takes over. "Are we to believe that boiling water soaks into a grit faster in your kitchen than in any place on the face of the earth? Perhaps the laws of physics cease to exist on your stove? Were these magic grits? Did you buy them from the same guy who sold Jack his beanstalk beans?"

The prosecutor's loud objection is sustained, but Vinnie keeps up the pressure.

"Are you sure about those five minutes?" as he raises his voice.

"I don't know."

"Are you sure about those five minutes?" Shouting now.

"I may have been mistaken."

"I got no more use for this guy," crows Vinnie in triumph.

Scorn and sarcasm worked well on Tipton, because the witness deserved it; he was clearly doing everything he could to help the prosecution, which gave Vinnie license to lace into him. But that approach could not work at all with the next witness, a prim, elderly African-American lady named Constance Riley. She is absolutely sincere in her identification of Bill and Stan, though it is evident that she can hardly see a thing without her glasses.

Vinnie begins his cross-examination politely. "Mrs. Riley, when you saw the defendants were you wearing your glasses?" The witness hesitates, scanning the courtroom. "Over here, dear," he adds helpfully.

"Yes, I was," replies Mrs. Riley, turning her head toward counsel.

"Would you mind putting your glasses on for us, please?"

She complies, removing a heavy set of glasses from her pocketbook and placing them on her face.

"Whoa!" exclaims Vinnie, "how long have you been wearing glasses?"

"Since I was six."

"Have they always been that thick?"

"Oh no, they got thicker over the years."

"So as you've gotten older, how many levels of thickness have you gone through?"

"Oh, I don't know. Over 60 years, maybe ten times."

"Maybe you're ready for a thicker set?"

"Oh no, I think they're okay."

"Maybe we should make sure. Let's check it out," suggests Vinnie, producing a large tape measure. "Now how far were the defendants from you when you saw them entering the Sac-O-Suds?"

"About 100 feet."

Vinnie hands Mrs. Riley one end of the tape measure and then backs away from her until he is standing at the far end of the courtroom. "Okay, this is 50 feet, half the distance," he says. "How many fingers am I holding up?"

The witness peers into the distance, squinting earnestly. "Four," she guesses.

Vinnie walks slowly toward her, past the jury box, keeping his hand in the air, showing two fingers.

"What do you think now, dear?" he asks courteously, once he is within her sight.

"I'm thinking of getting thicker lenses," she replies.

Vinnie made his point without embarrassing an honest, though mistaken, witness. The jury loved it, and I have it on good authority that Glen Kanwit agrees.

LESSON 8: *Beginner's Luck*

It's an old joke, with a punchline so instantly familiar that it works even without the original Yiddish accent.

"Pardon me, sir," says the youngster, a newcomer in New York, walking up to an elderly gentleman. "Can you tell me how to get to Carnegie Hall?"

"Practice."

It is utterly true, of course, in both poker and law, that success does not come easily. Skills are perfected and honed through years of hard work, often developed during low-pressure apprenticeships in environments such as small-stakes card games or relatively modest cases. Anyone who attempts to start at the top is looking for a hard fall, with seasoned veterans ready and waiting to take advantage of every slip-up or miscue.

Still, the myth of the gifted amateur endures—the novice who, through a combination of rare talent and kind providence, manages to outplay his betters and press home to victory.

That is the premise of *My Cousin Vinnie*, in which the eponymous protagonist manages to win a capital murder case, without ever before having set foot in a courtroom. He is confident he can do it, and so is his nephew, whose life is on the line. Why? Because all of the Gambinis are great at arguing, which can only mean that Vinnie is a born lawyer. Since the movie is a comedy, no one expresses much concern that Vinnie flunked the bar five times and has only been a lawyer for six weeks, or that he has to lie to the judge in order to be admitted *pro hac vice*. It doesn't seem to matter that he knows nothing about procedure—he didn't study it in law school, and he never got around to observing any legal proceedings while he worked as an auto mechanic and studied (and studied) for the bar—and even less about the Alabama practice rules. Vinnie has the one quality that counts—an innate ability to cut to the heart of an issue, dragging the truth out of reluctant witnesses and spotting the flaws in the other side's case.

It is that preternatural skill that ultimately saves the day for the defendants. When all seems lost, as the prosecution has produced a surprise witness who plugs the gaps in its case, Vinnie has an epiphany. Looking at a photograph of the tire tracks left by the true murderers' getaway car, he realizes that they could not have been made by Bill and Stan's car. Only a vehicle with "positraction" could have produced such even tracks, and that feature was not available on Bill and Stan's "faded metallic mint green 1964 Buick Skylark convertible."

Vinnie still needs an expert witness to establish his point, but—holy cow!—he just happens to have one. His girlfriend, Lisa, an unemployed hairdresser, just happens to be an automotive genius, having grown up surrounded by mechanics in her father's garage. She takes the stand and testifies so compellingly that the prosecutor gives an "aw shucks" smile—he is a good old boy, after all—and dismisses all the charges. Vinnie has won his first case. Handshakes all around, warm hugs and congratulations. He drives off with Lisa, planning their wedding and ready for the next challenge.

It is a wonderful film, perhaps the greatest courtroom comedy of all time, but its resolution bears only a passing resemblance to reality. Cases are never won by flashes of inspiration at the last moment, much less by miraculously available surprise witnesses, much less by fledgling lawyers who have never been in court. Deus ex machina may work in literature, but not in law.

And it doesn't work in poker either, at least not often. Vinnie's winning play was a lot like filling an inside straight on the river. It might happen now and then (more often in poker than in court), but it is not the sort of thing that you would want to bet your cousin's life on.

On the other hand, you might want to take a chance if you are playing with your own money. That is what Chris Moneymaker did in 2003, when he entered a $40 Internet poker tournament, where the ultimate prize was a seat (and the $10,000 buy-in) at the World Series of Poker at Binion's Horseshoe. Moneymaker (yes, that is his real name) won the preliminary tournament and flew to Las Vegas to compete against the most fabled names in professional poker. Although he was strictly an amateur—he had never before played in a live poker tournament—he ended up winning the whole thing, along with $2.5 million in prize money.

The 2003 WSOP was heavily covered by ESPN, so Chris Moneymaker eventually became a household name, at least in households that follow poker on cable television. He has also written a book called *Moneymaker: How an Amateur Poker Player Turned $40 into $2.5 Million at the World Series of Poker*, in which he provides a nearly hand-by-hand description of his remarkable run. To Moneymaker's great credit, he concedes that he benefited from many lucky draws, and he is unsparing in detailing the hands he misplayed, including several that almost brought him to disaster.

On his way to the final table, Moneymaker found himself going head to head with Humberto Brenes of Costa Rica, one of the best players in the world. Moneymaker had badly misread Brenes's hand, believing that the Costa Rican was on a draw when he was really holding pocket aces. "I was getting seriously outplayed," observed Moneymaker in retrospect, but thinking that he held the better hand (pocket eights), Chris went all in:

> Brenes watched me push my chips to the center of the table and his smile grew wide enough to accept mail. Then he called, and he waved his finger at me in a *tsk-tsk* gesture, like a grown-up catching a child with his hand in the cookie jar. Which is exactly what he had just done.
>
> I knew I was in trouble, but when he turned over those aces, I thought I'd die. I stood and stepped back from the table myself, calling out for an eight. And, sure enough, an eight came on the turn. It was the most remarkable thing. I thought, How about that! I was standing and praying . . . and an eight came along to bail me out. I jumped up and down and hugged

a couple guys along the rail I didn't even know and threw my fist in the air like I'd just won the lottery—which in a way I had, because there wasn't a whole lot of skill in how I'd just played this hand. This was the luck of the draw, and I didn't mind the outcome even as I hated the hard road I'd taken to it.

I'd been beat, made a devastatingly bad read, but the cards had smiled on me, and I let myself think that anytime you get outplayed and still come away with the pot, it's a good hand. At least you talk yourself into *believing* it's still a good hand.

His victory in the WSOP was not pure luck. Moneymaker brought some serious skills to the table, and he managed to outplay more than a few heavy-hitting professionals. Still, the impact of his surprising victory was probably summed up best by A. J. Jacobs, writing in the *New York Times*:

I have a feeling that the professional poker players threw the 2003 World Series of Poker. They held a meeting, took a vote and decided to let this accountant from Tennessee who'd never entered a live tournament walk away with the $2.5 million first prize. If so, it was a clever business move, a smart bet. Because now, every schlemiel with a pair of mirrored sunglasses and a rudimentary grasp of the rules of poker thinks he can play cards with the pros. And you can be sure 99.9 percent of them will leave with drained wallets and the sound of snickering in their ears.

Yes, lightning strikes now and then. Some games can be won through a combination of luck and good intentions. But only sometimes, and neither reliably nor often. Jacobs aptly described Moneymaker's book as "240 pages of false hope. It may cost $23.95, but I have a hunch it will cause more people to lose more money than any other book this year."

And Chris Moneymaker? He returned to the World Series of Poker the following year, no longer an unknown amateur but now the defending champion, presumably putting up the full $10,000 entry fee. But this time, fortune did not smile. Though now a professional, he misplayed a series of early hands—"where I tried to bully the other players a little too much, where I tried to raise a little too much, where I tried to reraise a little too much"—and soon found himself in a deep hole.

> I was easy picking, here on in, and I nursed my few remaining chips like they were all-important. I'd gotten to that place in my thinking where the tournament itself was no big deal, where posting that good showing I'd dreamed about for the past twelve months now took a backseat to getting some sleep. And it's been my admittedly limited experience that when you're resigned to losing there's nothing left to do but lose.

Chris Moneymaker was among the first players to be eliminated at the 2004 WSOP. We can only wonder about what happened in Vinnie Gambini's second case.

LESSON 9: *You Gotta Have Heart*

When card players talk about heart, they really mean courage or nerve or, more precisely, the ability to trust your own judgment even at the risk of losing everything. It is a peculiar conception of heart, placing composure ahead of compassion. Some might even call it coldheartedness (card players themselves refer approvingly to "alligator blood"), although there is a certain nobility in a poker player's willingness to accept total defeat at the turn of a card.

Heart means backing your own play, staying calm when the stakes are enormous, maintaining equanimity when the poker gods frown, and accepting bad beats as part of the game. Because everyone strives to show heart, there is no need to pity the losers, so long as they wagered bravely (nor is there any need to pity the suckers, who got what they deserved). It is a convenient concept because it justifies, even idealizes, the most merciless—and therefore crucial—aspects of the game.

Amateurs who stick to friendly games do not need much heart, but it is absolutely essential to professionals. The poet Katy Lederer learned all about heart when she briefly attempted to master poker under the guidance of her older siblings, Howard and Annie, who were two of the most successful professionals in Las Vegas. In her memoir, *Poker Face*, she tells the story of one critical lesson from her sister.

"I remember this guy," said Annie, "he sat down at my table just the other night. He was in his mid-twenties, a little bit older than you, and he put down two full racks of hundreds—it was twenty thousand dollars altogether—and I'd never seen him before."

"That seems weird," said Katy.

"It *was* weird," Annie replied. "Highly unusual. And he didn't look like anyone who'd have a lot of money. He explained that he'd sold off his jeans in the morning—for ten or twenty dollars—and then played a full day straight before getting to [the high-limit, seven-card stud] table, which wasn't any place he should have been."

"So the guy was no good, but he went on some streak?"

"That's right, and he didn't even have his jeans any more. He was wearing these old, worn-out khakis, and he was sitting there across from me at the table, looking lost."

"Shouldn't he have known better?" Katy asked. "Shouldn't he have taken all those hundred-dollar chips and put them on a car or on a house?"

"But that's how things work," Annie explained. "For the guy to have amassed the twenty thousand dollars in the first place means he was a maniac. People just aren't rational."

"So what happened?"

"So this guy was now across from me," continued Annie, "and the dealer deals me perfect eights, I got rolled up eights." In seven-card stud, "rolled up" means that the player's first three cards make three of a kind. "I have these great trips, but the guy can see only the one eight that's showing, so I play him for all he's worth, and he loses twenty thousand dollars then and there."

That was Annie's story. Then came the lesson for her little sister.

"And I wouldn't say I felt bad, because that's just not how I felt, but it wasn't a pleasant thing to take money from such a clueless person. And I just can't see you being happy having to make that decision again and again, like Howard and I have to do—to take someone's money, even if they do happen to be a total *moron*."

In the end, that's all there is to serious poker—taking money from people who are willing to lose it. Sure, there is plenty of skill, and some measure of passing enjoyment, but in the end it is completely unproductive.

Law practice, on the other hand, is never completely divorced from justice. Often we do not see the underlying utility of lawyering, and justice too frequently eludes us. But the purpose of law practice, for all of its many imperfections, is essentially admirable. At our best, lawyers facilitate autonomy—for individuals, organizations, businesses, and "the people"—which is the ultimate cornerstone of prosperity, security, and liberty. Although we may not often achieve our ideals, there is room in the law for zeal, compassion, dedication, commitment, loyalty, trust, integrity, forbearance, devotion, and honor. Some lawyers never quite get the point, treating law practice, à la Joe Dowd, like a poker game—but when most of us say "heart," we mean it.

LESSON 10: *Cards Speak*

You can disguise your hand as long as the betting continues, representing cards that you don't have or hiding your true strength. If no one calls, you can keep your secrets forever. But when there is a showdown—the last bet is called—everyone has to put their cards on the table, face up. And then the cards speak. They are what they are, without regard to any of the previous bluffs, disguises, false fronts, or mistaken impressions. That is the underlying ethic of poker, on which the integrity of the game depends. When the bets are called, the best cards always win.

Poker players take much pride in the cards-speak rule, and the righteous way they adhere to it, even when it costs them money. Anthony Holden tells a story about a player

nicknamed after a good luck charm. Holden was dealt A♠
6♠, and the flop was 5♠ 7♦ 8♠. With both an open-ended
straight and a flush draw, he bet heavily—and he was called
by a player who kept a rabbit's foot next to his stack. The turn
brought 9♠, completing Holden's straight (while he still had
the nut flush draw). With no pairs showing, the only pocket
cards that could beat him at that point were 10 J (making a
higher straight), so Holden kept betting. The river brought
10♣, causing Holden to hold his breath momentarily when
he contemplated the open-ended straight draw—7♦ 8♠ 9♥
10♣—on the board. Rabbit's Foot checked, however, so
Holden bet all of his remaining chips. To his surprise, Rabbit's Foot called, setting them both all in:

> When I showed my straight, Rabbit's Foot threw away
> his cards; but they flipped over just short of the muck
> to reveal a pair of jacks. The dealer took a long, slow
> look at them while the loser shrugged his shoulders,
> picked up his rabbit's foot and prepared to leave. He
> thought he had a pair of jacks. In fact, he had wound
> up with a straight higher than mine. At this game, as
> they say, "cards speak," so the dealer did his duty and
> pointed out to the departing stranger that he had just
> won a pot.

"Ah well, them's the breaks," said Holden. In poker,
you are free to take ruthless advantage of your opponents'
mistakes, unless they call your last bet. At that point, the
cards take over, and mistakes don't matter. Although it may
be hard to believe, it seems that players misread their own
hands (failing to recognize winners) with some frequency,
even at the highest level of play. James McManus saw it
happen twice at the 2000 World Series of Poker, including

once when the dealer—who is supposed to announce the winner—made the mistake as well, and the hand had to be reconstructed after the error was pointed out by a spectator. Almost every poker book tells a similar story, always with the same moral.

It is fascinating that card players are so dedicated to the cards-speak principle, since a contrary rule would make just as much sense. In every other regard, poker adheres to a pitiless code of Social Darwinism. You act strictly at your own peril, taking full responsibility for your errors and omissions. It would be easy to imagine a standard under which you must accurately announce your hand's rank, suffering the consequences if you read it incorrectly. But no. Its universally recognized face value is immutable, whether recognized by the player, the dealer, or the spectators.

There are numerous examples in law practice where integrity trumps tactical advantage. The most obvious is the jury poll, when the judge asks each juror individually to confirm that he or she voted for the announced verdict. It is essential to ensure that the verdict entered is the one that the jury truly voted, not merely the one announced by the foreperson. It is unusual for a poll to upset a verdict (much less common, apparently, than a misread poker hand), but it has been known to happen.

To the credit of our profession, lawyers are increasingly called upon to forgo accidental advantages. Consider, for example, the problem of privileged materials that are inadvertently disclosed during discovery. The traditional rule was that accidental publication destroyed any privilege and that the recipient of such documents was free to use them. With the advent of massive litigation, sometimes involving hundreds of thousands of pages, not to mention electronic discovery, it became apparent that there could be no absolute safeguard against the inadvertent distribution of privileged documents. Consequently, nearly all jurisdictions prohibit lawyers from simply exploiting an adversary's mistaken production. At a minimum, you must segregate any material that appears to be privileged, until you can determine whether the privilege has been waived. Some jurisdictions go even further, requiring that such documents simply be returned unread.

On the other hand, lawyers remain free to pounce on and exploit all manner of blunders by the opposition. We may vigorously cross-examine confused and forgetful (but truthful) witnesses, in order to undermine their testimony. We may move to dismiss when the other side misses a deadline, no matter how meritorious their case. At the worst extreme, the appellate waiver doctrine can be invoked to prevent wrongly convicted defendants from asserting their claims in habeas corpus petitions, while prosecutors keep mum.

To be sure, the adversary system presupposes a certain amount of jockeying and gamesmanship—some of it implicit in the concepts of due process and the Fifth Amendment. Nonetheless, we might all be better off if we had to let the cards speak more often.

LESSON 11: *Cross-Examination Does Not Mean Angry Examination*

If the top poker players agree about anything, it is the value of relentless aggression. Many lawyers would say the same thing, justifying their ready resort to roughshod tactics. As usual, the card players know what they are talking about.

And so do some of the lawyers, although, as we will see, effective aggression is not at all the same thing as belligerence.

As Doyle Brunson notes, "The very best players I know are extremely aggressive," constantly trying to take control of the game by betting and raising against their weaker (meaning more timid) opponents. Some aggressive players can be obnoxious, or even nasty, but that is far from necessary. Indeed, an aggressive card player can be courteous, or even courtly, while simultaneously intimidating his opponents into throwing away their hands.

Brunson's point is that his aggressive betting creates risk for the other players, making them inclined to back down by folding their hands. This allows him to win numerous small pots with inferior cards, because no one is willing to pay the increasingly steep price to see his hand. Someone who plays back at Brunson (calling his bet or, worse, raising him) is likely to be set all in, putting his entire stack in jeopardy. Realizing this, only players with the nuts (or close to it) are likely to bet against Brunson. And since the nuts do not show up very often, he tends to win by default most of the time.

It is an elegant strategy, capitalizing on the flow of the game and the inherently conservative nature of all but the very best players. Poker typically rewards tight play and careful hand selection, but Brunson has discovered a way to exploit what would otherwise be his opponents' strengths: "A very big part of winning consistently . . . is to get the other guy in a position where if he makes a bet he's actually jeopardizing all his chips as opposed to you jeopardizing all of yours."

Brunson's reputation for massive reraises makes every opponent hesitant to call, wary that the bets will only get bigger until everything is on the table. By taking the initiative, therefore, Brunson leverages his initial bets with the implicit threat that there will be more to come. He gives the example of playing against an opponent who has a $20,000 stack. Brunson's opening bet of $7,000 implies additional raises to come, so the other player actually has to consider whether his hand is worth risking his entire $20,000. "You're betting seven thousand," Brunson explains, "he's betting twenty."

> I always try to make the bet that puts him in jeopardy . . . not me. If he's right . . . and I'm bluffing . . . he's going to move in with his twenty thousand—and I'm not going to call him. So he'll win seven thousand. But, if he's wrong . . . and I've got a hand . . . he's still going to move in. But now he's going to get called—and he's going to lose twenty thousand.
>
> So he's laying me about 3 to 1—his twenty thousand to my seven. I put the commitment on him. I make him commit himself. I'm **not** committed. Whether he thinks I am or not . . . I'm not. That's the beauty of it. He's thinking about my bet . . . and wondering how much more he's going to have to put in there.
>
> It's an either/or situation. Either I'm bluffing . . . or I've got the nuts. And against me, he knows it **could** cost him twenty thousand—his whole stack—unless he throws his hand away.

The logical response is almost always to fold—"Take it, Doyle; take it, Doyle"—which gives Brunson an enormous advantage, whether his cards are good or mediocre.

Litigators are often criticized for being too aggressive, which really means that they act like jerks—trying to bash or bully their adversaries, witnesses, or even the courts. That sort of aggression is usually pointless. It seldom results in submission, and it often leads to payback in kind. There is another type of aggression, however, à la Brunson, that can work wonders. Let's call it "initiative" or "momentum," meaning that you take extreme advantage of the first move.

There is a central dilemma in litigation. Memory is visual, but communication is verbal. A witness does not remember events in words, but rather in images that cannot be transferred intact to the fact finder. Instead, the witness's recollections must first be put into words, in the hope that the listeners (judge or jury) will visualize the same scenes with some degree of accuracy. When language is artful, it is possible that the jury will reimagine the events consistently with the lawyer's own vision.

Every trial, therefore, becomes a battle for imagination, as each side attempts to influence the way that the jurors envision the key events. And here, the advantage belongs to the lawyer who can seize the initiative by drawing the boldest, clearest, most-compelling picture of the case. It helps to go first, of course, but it helps even more to be vivid, creative, and venturesome—one might even say aggressive—in telling the story.

The opening moment is essential, because jurors (and judges, too) will almost certainly jump to conclusions at every stage of the trial (not only in opening statements, but during witness examinations and final argument as well). This is contrary to the standard legal conception of juror decision making—in which individuals receive information in strictly linear fashion, first one discrete fact and then another, withholding judgment until the very end of the case—but it is well supported by cognition science. In reality, people tend to reach conclusions quickly, making some pre-liminary decisions almost immediately. Psychologists refer to this phenomenon as "scripting" or "framing," meaning that an individual almost always attempts to make sense of new information by fitting it into her preexisting knowledge base through the use of familiar frames.

To take the simplest of examples, suppose that a witness testified about the robbery of a hardware store. Before hear-ing another word, each juror would begin to imagine a famil-iar hardware store setting, with checkout aisles, a customer service counter, and various plumbing, tool, and electrical departments. The image would be refined, of course, by addi-tional testimony, perhaps describing the store as either a big-box chain or a local mom-and-pop operation. But even then, the jurors would continue the process of instant framing. To a suburban juror, even a neighborhood store would probably have a parking lot, which might lead to other conclusions, say, about the location of a getaway car.

In other words, new information is quickly harmonized with existing knowledge, which allows us to make sense of the world. While jumping to conclusions is often disparaged, especially by judges, it is actually hardwired in our genetic code. Thus, the initial picture of a case can be enormously powerful, heavily influencing every conclusion that the jury draws thereafter. A lawyer must therefore be aggressive—meaning assertive, not hostile—in presenting such a picture to the jury, as quickly and as strongly as possible.

A splendid example of the framing phenomenon can be seen in the musical comedy *The Music Man*. Professor Harold Hill (in truth a slick traveling salesman) arrives in the naive town of River City, Iowa, determined to make a bundle by selling band instruments to the unwary rubes. Unfortu-

nately for him, the local citizens have no particular interest in horns and flutes, so Hill first has to convince them
that they need to establish a boys' band. Well, he explains,
the young men of River City are in great jeopardy, virtually
on the verge of delinquency, because a pool hall recently
opened in town. "My friends, you've got trouble," he warns
them. "With a capital *T* and that rhymes with *p* and that
stands for *pool*!"

In Hill's narrative, the pool hall becomes a story frame,
symbolizing degeneracy and crime. It is a dark, smoky, and
disreputable place where children are in constant danger
of being lured into lives of dissolution and worse. Only a
wholesome, healthy alternative can save them. Yes, that is
what they need. A marching band!

The story worked because of its imagery. The frame successfully raised the fears of the townsfolk, who were ready
to assume the wickedness of a pool hall. But what would
have happened if Hill had tried a different frame? "You've
got trouble with a capital *T* and that rhymes with *b* and that
stands for billiards." He would have gone home broke, unable
to sell a single trumpet or trombone, because a billiard parlor—formal, well-lighted, genteel—just does not evoke the
same foreboding.

Hill was charming, even delightful, in his pitch to the citizens of River City. But he was also aggressive, pushing his
plan as hard as he could. And more than that—in a way that
Doyle Brunson would recognize—he convinced the townsfolk that they were actually at great risk if they did not give
him their money. "Take it, Harold, take it!"

Frame theory provides many equally powerful tools for
litigators. Most important is the understanding that the
story itself, conceived as a whole, is far more meaningful than

any of its constituent facts. Jurors do not accumulate facts in order to arrive at a story. Instead, jurors begin to imagine a story almost immediately, interpreting subsequent facts to fit into the familiar frame.

This, in turn, explains many of the proven techniques of trial advocacy. For example, most lawyers recognize the need to start strong by putting the most important information near the beginning of every argument and witness examination. The usual rationale, sometimes called the concept of "primacy," is that jurors best remember those things that they hear first. In fact, frame theory tells us that initiative is even more crucial, because that first image can be used to influence the way that all subsequent information will be received.

Doyle Brunson probably doesn't care about cognition science or framing theory, but he obviously knows how they work. By developing his image as an aggressive player, he causes his opponents to jump to conclusions on every hand. Lawyers can do more or less the same, by capturing the jury's attention and imagination with a strong primary story. That may not seem as hard-hitting as yelling at an adversary or looming over a witness, but it is more effective and therefore more aggressive.

LESSON 12: *Beautiful Losers*

In perhaps the most famous opening line in all of Russian literature, Leo Tolstoy observed that "happy families are all alike; but every unhappy family is unhappy in its own way." *Anna Karenina* continues for nearly another 1,000 pages, exploring grand themes of love and betrayal. Some of the characters manage to find a bit of contentment in their tangled affairs, but it is the heartbreak, the sorrow, that moves the story forward. There is no great literature about happy families, because happiness is uninteresting and, worse, there is almost nothing we can learn from it. To increase our knowledge, to deepen our understanding of the human condition, we must instead turn our attention to grief. That is why physicians study pathology, engineers study disasters, psychologists study psychoses, and card players endlessly replay lost hands. It can be helpful to identify the things you did right, but it is critical to recognize how things went wrong.

The great virtue of Chris Moneymaker's book about his unlikely victory in the 2003 World Series of Poker is its candid appraisal of his misplays and blunders. After all, there is not much we can learn about winning the tournament, except that amateurs occasionally get lucky. We can learn a lot, however, from Moneymaker's clear description of the fumbled hands that he would play differently if he had it to do over again. That is how you improve, of course, learning how to correct your errors.

In one hand toward the end of the tournament, Moneymaker found himself holding an ace and a king before the flop. Howard Lederer made a large bet of $40,000, which Moneymaker called—"because when you've got the chips to back it up, you've got to play those ace-king hole cards." That was a decision he would shortly regret.

> The flop was just rags—low cards that didn't do a single thing for me, nor (I was betting) for Lederer, but Lederer came back with another 40,000 raise, which I had to call. There was no help on the turn, but I

figured I'd make a play for the pot. I'd thrown about 100,000 in chips into this one pot, and now I pushed in another 90,000, hoping to push Lederer off the hand in the bargain. But he pushed back—all in. And I was stuck. I'd committed almost 200,000 in chips at a time when I wasn't planning on getting mixed up in anything big, and here I was thinking about committing some 200,000 more. I thought about it, and I thought about it, and I thought about it, all the way to forever, until I finally folded.

Lederer didn't have to show me his cards, but he did: pocket queens. He had me. I'd made the right call, but he'd made the right play, and it ended up costing me a whole mess of chips.

Yes, Moneymaker made the right call at the end, but it did not take great skill to fold his ace-high rag hand—which would have been beaten by any small pair—rather than call a $200,000 bet. The real lesson, as Moneymaker points out, is that he should have folder earlier, rather than trying to push Lederer off a good hand. In other words, we can learn more from his bad decision than from his good one.

The same holds true for litigation. We can often benefit most by learning how a case was lost. In the perjury case against Martha Stewart, for example, the prosecutors had a strong hand, and they played it well. The charges against Stewart were straightforward, with witnesses ready to testify that the popular, proper, elegant defendant had lied to Securities and Exchange Commission investigators about the sale of a small amount of ImClone stock.

Still, it would not have been enough merely to tell the jurors that Martha Stewart lied about her conversation with her stockbroker. They had to be able to envision her talking on the phone with the young man, nodding as he explained the imminent decline in ImClone's share price, giving him the fatal instruction, and then betraying her hard-won persona by brazenly lying to the SEC investigators. Without visualization, there could be no conviction. The prosecutors had to recreate Martha Stewart's image, changing her from a perfectionist homemaking maven to a greedy liar, and they had to do it through the secondhand description of events that the jury would never see.

This is a familiar task for successful trial lawyers. In the Stewart case, the prosecutors met the challenge by calling upon witnesses to describe Stewart's venal side—depicting her as demanding, egotistical, and self-centered—so that the jurors could envision her as exactly the sort of person who would eagerly take advantage of an inside tip and then arrogantly attempt to conceal the deed. They played a tape-recorded interview with her codefendant, her stockbroker Peter Bacanovic, in which he described his most important client as "someone who gets irascible" about her portfolio, and they introduced an e-mail in which she threatened to withdraw her account and "give my money to a professional money manager who will watch it when I am too busy."

Most significantly, the prosecutors repeatedly illustrated their case with revealing vignettes, including a description of Martha Stewart and Peter Bacanovic posing for a photograph in pink and blue bathrobes. After that, it would be significantly easier for the jury to imagine that Stewart and Bacanovic had a relationship that went beyond stockbrokering, one in which they might conspire to dump stock and cover up the details.

The prosecution case was nicely presented, but it was nothing out of the ordinary. Marshal your witnesses and get them to testify in vivid terms, presenting evidence that supports your key allegations. Well, duh.

The more fascinating question is not how the prosecutors assembled their case, but how Martha Stewart managed to lose. Her lawyers, after all, could call on significant resources. As a media figure, Stewart had built an international business empire by establishing a reputation for dependability. Hundreds of thousands—perhaps millions—of consumers knew that they could trust Martha Stewart on matters of good taste and discernment. Could 12 jurors really be convinced to brand her a fraud?

Moreover, there was actually only one witness who could provide direct evidence that Martha Stewart lied. Douglas Faneuil, a 28-year-old assistant stockbroker at Merrill Lynch, testified that he alerted Stewart to the impending decline of her stock in ImClone and that she ordered him to sell her holdings based on that tip. Stewart had denied those same facts in two interviews with investigators from the SEC, and that contradiction formed the basis of the case against her.

Faneuil, however, had grave credibility problems. His admitted conduct—tipping off a client based on inside information—was far more serious than anything attributed to Martha Stewart, yet he was testifying under a deal that allowed him to plead guilty only to a misdemeanor. Moreover, he had no way of controverting Stewart's defense, that she actually sold the stock pursuant to a prearranged sell order with Faneuil's boss, Peter Bacanovic. In a believability contest, the iconic Stewart started with a significant advantage over the callow Faneuil, and the lawyers all knew it.

So the story of Stewart's integrity was there to be told, in sharp contrast to the prosecution's graphic depiction of guilt. And defense counsel responded by painting a picture of, well, nothing. As Jeffrey Toobin observed in the *New Yorker*, in the entire five-week trial, the defense offered only about three sentences that stressed Stewart's good deeds and accomplishments. Stewart did not testify in her own behalf, and her lawyer produced only one witness on a relatively minor point. Now, there are many good reasons for keeping a defendant off the stand, and Stewart's attorneys can no doubt provide an excellent explanation for their strategy. The cost of silence, however, can be enormous, leaving the jury with a strong visual impression of guilt but with no way to envision an "innocence" story.

Presenting your strongest evidence is an obvious choice, so you could probably say that all happy prosecutors are alike. But keeping a popular, well-spoken, attractive client off the stand is a much tougher decision that has the potential to backfire badly, which makes it far more instructive. As Martha Stewart learned to her dismay, every convicted defendant loses in her own special way.

LESSON 13: *Poker Ain't Life*

You can bet on it.

Rank of Hands

A♠ K♠ Q♠ J♠ 10♠	Royal Flush
9♥ 8♥ 7♥ 6♥ 5♥	Straight Flush
8♣ 8♦ 8♥ 8♠ 2♦	Four of a Kind
Q♦ Q♥ Q♠ 6♣ 6♥	Full House
J♦ 8♦ 6♦ 5♦ 3♦	Flush
8♥ 7♣ 6♦ 5♦ 4♠	Straight
10♦ 10♠ 10♣ K♥ J♥	Three of a Kind
K♥ K♣ 4♦ 4♣ 7♣	Two Pair
9♣ 9♦ Q♣ 8♥ 5♠	One Pair
A♥ 10♥ 7♥ 4♣ 2♥	High Card

Glossary

Ante. Small amount of money put into the pot by each player at the beginning of every hand.

Blank. Small or useless card (also called a rag).

Blind. Mandatory bet to open the hand; often the first two players must make bets of different values ("big blind" and "little blind") before they see their cards.

Bluff. Aggressive betting on a mediocre-to-nonexistent hand for the purpose of causing other players to fold.

Board. Cards that are dealt face up.

Busted hand. Drawing hand (potential straight or flush) that is never completed.

Button. In a game with a professional dealer, a marker that is passed clockwise to indicate the nominal dealer for the purpose of determining the order of betting.

Call. Matching another player's bet without raising it.

Chasing. Continuing to play in the hope of drawing favorable cards when the odds are poor.

Check. Declining an opportunity to make the first bet.

Community cards. In Texas Hold'em, the cards dealt face up that can be used by every player.

Deal seconds. Form of deck manipulation; holding onto the top card, so that it can be given to a confederate, while dealing the second one instead.

Deck mechanic. Cheater who surreptitiously arranges the deck.

Draw. (1) Taking cards; (2) a poker game in which each player is initially given five cards.

Drawing hand. Incomplete straight or flush that may be improved by additional cards.

Early position. In Texas Hold'em, the first few players to the left of the dealer or button.

Fifth street. (1) In Texas Hold'em, the fifth communal card, dealt face up (also called the river); (2) in stud games, the fifth card dealt to each remaining player.

Flop. First three communal cards in Texas Hold'em, dealt face up.

Flush. Five cards of the same suit.

Fold. To discard your hand by declining to match another player's bet.

Four flush. Four cards of the same suit.

Fourth street. (1) In Texas Hold'em, the fourth communal card, dealt face up (also called the turn); (2) in stud games, the fourth card dealt to each remaining player.

Full house. Three of a kind plus a pair.

Grinding. Playing consistently at low or moderate stakes to "grind out" a constant profit; applies primarily to professional players.

High-low split. Poker game in which the high hand divides the pot with the lowest hand, usually (though not always) consisting of all unmatched cards.

Hole cards. Cards dealt face down in Texas Hold'em or stud poker.

Inside straight draw. Four cards comprising a potential straight, with the missing card somewhere in the middle, as in 9-10-Q-K or 4-6-7-8.

Kicker. Next highest card, which is used to break a tie when two players otherwise have hands of the same value.

Late position. In Texas Hold'em, the players farthest to the left of the dealer or button.

Limp in. (1) In Texas Hold'em, to call the big blind without raising; (2) to call any first bet.

Loose play. Consistently betting (or calling) with unfavorable odds.

Made hand. Completed hand that does not need to be improved by additional cards; a straight or better.

Manipulator. Cheat who surreptitiously arranges the deck.

Mechanic. Cheat who surreptitiously arranges the deck.

Muck. (1) Pile of discards; (2) to throw away or discard your hand.

Nuts. (1) Hand that is certain to win; (2) the best possible hand at that point in the game.

Open. Make the first bet.

Open-ended straight draw. Four sequential cards comprising a potential straight, with missing cards at either end, as in 8-9-10-J.

Outs. Cards that will improve your hand.

Pair. Two cards of the same rank.

Pocket cards. Cards dealt face down in Texas Hold'em or stud poker.

Pot. Money that has already been wagered, which is placed in the middle of the table.

Pot odds. Relationship between the total amount of money in the pot and the amount necessary to call a bet or raise.

Premium hand. Very good starting hand.

Quads. Four of a kind.

Rag. Small or useless card (also called a blank).

Rag hand. Very poor hand unlikely to be improved by additional cards.

Rainbow. Three cards of different suits.

Raise. (1) Make an initial bet or increase another player's earlier bet; (2) the amount of a bet or raise.

Representing a hand. Creating the impression that you hold a particular hand.

River. (1) Fifth and final communal card in Texas Hold'em, dealt face up (also called fifth street); (2) in other games, the last card dealt.

Rolled up. In seven-card stud, getting three of a kind (two down and one up) on the first three cards.

Royal flush. Ten through ace of the same suit.

Semi-bluff. Raising with a potential but not yet completed hand.

Set. Three cards of the same rank, when two are face down and the third is on the board.

Shorting the pot. Cheating by throwing fewer chips than called for into the pot.

Slow playing. Declining to bet heavily on a strong hand, in the hope of drawing more money into the pot.

Splash the pot. Rudely throwing chips into the pot so that they scatter, making it impossible to determine whether the bet was short.

Stacked deck. Deck that has been manipulated or arranged by a cheater.

Steaming. Playing badly and making poor decisions, usually brought on by losing (also called going on tilt).

Straight. Five sequential cards of different suits.

Straight flush. Five sequential cards of the same suit.

String betting. Betting in a discontinuous action (without announcing the size of the bet) by throwing some chips into the pot while watching other players' reactions; usually considered against the rules.

Stud. Type of poker in which each player receives some cards face down and some face up. In five-card stud, each player receives one card face down and four face up; in seven-card stud, each player receives three cards face down (the first, second, and seventh) and four face up.

Suited. Cards of the same suit.

Tell. Unintentional gesture or expression that gives away a player's cards or intentions.

Texas Hold'em. Poker game in which each player receives two cards face down, followed by five face-up communal cards that can be used by everyone.

Three-flush. Three cards of the same suit.

Three of a kind. Three cards of the same rank.

Tight play. (1) Playing very few hands; (2) betting only on extremely good cards.

Tilt or going on tilt. Playing badly and making poor decisions, usually brought on by losing (also called steaming).

Trips. Three of a kind, comprising one hole card and two on the board.

Turn. Fourth communal card in Texas Hold'em, dealt face up (also called fourth street).

Under the gun. First player to act in a hand.

Up cards. Cards dealt face up in stud or Texas Hold'em.

NOTES

The young Texas lawyer was named Edward Fontaine Nicolds, and his story was related to me by his great-granddaughter, the California writer Sarah Stegall. Nicolds successfully practiced law in Texas for the rest of his life. He was later known in his family as "the judge," although there seems to be no record that he ever actually served on the bench. It is a family tradition, however, that he always maintained a suite of rooms at Austin's Driskill Hotel in order to play poker.

The James McManus quote is from *Positively Fifth Street*, p. 119.

DIAMONDS

The opening story about the Leopold and Loeb case is taken from Professor Douglas Linder's "Famous American Trials" Web site, http://www.law.umkc.edu/faculty/projects/ftrials/leoploeb/leopold.htm.

■

LESSON 1: *Saving Bets*

Some parts of this lesson, and the following one, were included in Steven Lubet, "Lawyers' Poker," *University of Miami Law Review* 57 (2003): 283. The observation about controlling chaos belongs to Larry Phillips, as he explains in *Zen and the Art of Poker*, p. 25.

LESSON 3: *Don't Gamble*

The definition of *gambling* is found in *Webster's New Universal Unabridged Dictionary*, 2d ed. (1983), p. 176. The quote from Anthony Holden—gambling is a "style" of playing poker—is from *Big Deal: One Year as a Professional Poker Player*, p. 180.

LESSON 4: *Depend on the Rabbit's Foot If You Will, but Remember: It Didn't Work for the Rabbit*

The title of this section is taken from Andy Bellin's *Poker Nation: A High-Stakes, Low-Life Adventure into the Heart of a Gambling Country*. The story of the Hiss trial, including the transcript of Dr. Binger's cross-examination, is taken from Douglas Linder's "Famous American Trials" Web site: http://www.law.umkc .edu/faculty/projects/ftrials/hiss/hiss.html.

LESSON 5: *Opening Hands*

The Ken Warren query about two-card contests is from *Winner's Guide to Texas Hold'em Poker*, p. 104.

LESSON 6: *Drawing Hands*

Doyle Brunson's observation about pocket aces comes from the original *Super System*, p. 388.

LESSON 7: *Chasing Is for Dogs*

There are many accounts of the marathon game between Nick the Greek and Johnny Moss. This one is adapted from Anthony Holden's *Big Deal*, pp. 41–43; and A. Alvarez's *Poker*, pp. 94–96.

The story of the Binion family is tragic, involving double-crosses, betrayals, adultery, drug addiction, financial ruin, and a murder prosecution. It is beautifully told in James McManus's *Positively Fifth Street*, although the tangled events continued in the years following McManus's publication.

Andy Bellin's quip is at p. 234 of *Poker Nation*. Amarillo Slim's colorful observation about amorous dogs is found on p. 253 of Anthony Holden's *Big Deal: One Year as a Professional Poker Player*.

LESSON 8: *Yardley's Law (and Darrow's Exception)*

Herbert O. Yardley's 1957 memoir is *The Education of a Poker Player*; his description of tight play is found on p. 52. Alvarez's characterization of Yardley's approach—"Assume the worst; believe no one"—is found on p. 29 of *Poker: Bets, Bluffs, and Bad Beats*.

The Scopes trial transcripts are from Professor Douglas Linder's "Famous American Trials" Web site, http://www.law.umkc.edu/faculty/projects/ftrials/scopes/scopes.htm.

LESSON 9: *Losing It*

Alvarez's observation about the length of the short run is from *Poker*, p. 61; the quotes from Puggy Pearson and Bobby Baldwin are from p. 51 of the same book. Andy Bellin's description of going on tilt is found on p. 131 of *Poker Nation*.

There are many versions of the famous Abraham Lincoln story. This iteration is adapted from the late Irving Younger's memorable videotaped lecture, *The Ten Commandments of Cross-Examination* (Basic Concepts in the Law of Evidence series, National Institute for Trial Advocacy).

The Rosenberg trial transcripts are from Professor Douglas Linder's "Famous American Trials" Web site, http://www.law.umkc.edu/faculty/projects/ftrials/rosenb/rosenb.htm.

LESSON 10: *Desperate Times*

■

Doyle Brunson's comment about learning how to lose is from *Super System*, p. 357. His account of playing the 10-2 combination is from Allyn Jaffrey Shulman, "Doyle Brunson: Five Decades of Poker and Still Going Strong," *Card Player Magazine*, August 27, 2004.

LESSON 11: *Volatility*

Doyle Brunson's preference for raising can be found in *Super System*, p. 503.

LESSON 12: *Sunk Costs*

David Sklansky's observation about the money in the pot—"no part of which belongs to you any longer"—is from his book *The Theory of Poker*, pp. 28–29. Anthony Holden agrees at p. 47 of *Big Deal*.

LESSON 13: *Stakes Matter*

Herbert Yardley's preference for small stakes is explained in the introduction (p. vii) of *The Education of a Poker Player*. Andy Bellin concurs, at least to the extent that he cautions against playing over your head (describing the treacherous seductiveness of betting with chips rather than money) at p. 121 of *Poker Nation*.

Alvarez's reference to the "graveyards of hometown champs" is found on p. 150 of *The Biggest Game in Town*, while his admiration for the imperturbability of elite players is expressed on pp. 43–44, and his description of chips as a "bag of beans" is found on pp. 46–47 of the same book. He further notes that their "imagination starts where logic falters" in *Poker*, p. 83.

Big Julie's insight—"the person who invented chips was a genius"—is part of poker folklore, eventually quoted in one form or another by most writers.

The quotes from the O. J. Simpson trial are from Professor Douglas Linder's "Famous American Trials" Web site, http:// www.law.umkc.edu/faculty/projects/ftrials/Simpson/simpson. htm. Johnnie Cochran's recollections are found in Johnnie Cochran, *Journey to Justice*, 299–300. Christopher Darden's account of the "bloody glove" demonstration is in his memoir, *In Contempt*, p. 323.

LESSON 1: *Fundamentalism*

David Sklansky's fundamental theorem of poker is found on pp. 17–18 of his book *The Theory of Poker*.

LESSON 2: *Know Why You Are Betting*

Bellin's typology of betting is explained on pp. 33–35 of *Poker Nation*, while Sklansky's elaboration is on p. 121 of *The Theory of Poker*. My trial advocacy text is *Modern Trial Advocacy*, 3d ed. (2004); the admonition against unnecessary impeachment is developed on pp. 153–58.

LESSON 3: *Slow Playing*

Yardley's anecdote about Monty's slow playing is on p. 37 of *The Education of a Poker Player*. Philip Beck frequently tells the story of slow playing the opposing expert witness in *Bush v. Gore* (2000), but it has not previously appeared in print (he confirmed it to me in an e-mail exchange).

LESSON 4: *Bluffing*

Bellin's explanation of bluffing is on pp. 76–80 of *Poker Nation*. Von Neumann and Morgenstern's classic text is *Theory of Games and Economic Behavior*; they expound on poker at pp. 188–89.

LESSON 5: *Reverse Bluffing*

Alvarez tells the story of Jack Strauss's masterful ploy on p. 67 of *Poker*.

LESSON 6: *Semi-Bluffing*

Semi-bluffing is defined by Sklansky on p. 91 of *The Theory of Poker*. The scope of discovery is defined by Rule 26(b), *Federal Rules of Civil Procedure*.

The excerpts from Oscar Wilde's trial are taken from *The Real Trial of Oscar Wilde*, edited by Merlin Holland, who is Wilde's grandson.

LESSON 7: *Overplaying*

Brunson's discussion of the folly of bluffing a poor player is found on pp. 433–34 of *Super System*; the italics, boldface, and ellipses are all in the original. Yardley's similar observation is on p. 19 of *The Education of a Poker Player*.

Alan Morrison's story about Merrill Williams has not been published; the quotes are from an e-mail that he sent me.

LESSON 9: *Loose Wiring*

The Law of Loose Wiring is explained in *Caro's Book of Tells*, pp. 47–49.

LESSON 10: *Folding Winners*

Alvarez quotes Amarillo Slim and tells the story of Doyle Brunson's magnificent retreat in *Poker*, p. 90.

The tragic events of the Amadou Diallo case are well known. More details can be found in Jeffrey Toobin's article in the *New Yorker*, "The Unasked Question: Why the Diallo Case Missed the Point," March 6, 2000, p. 38.

The Amarillo Slim anecdote was told by Alvarez in *The Biggest Game in Town*, p. 38.

LESSON 12: *Implication and Storytelling*

The best book on Bernhard Goetz is George Fletcher's *A Crime of Self-Defense: Bernhard Goetz and the Law on Trial.*

LESSON 13: *Patience*

The "patience" quote from James McManus is found in *Positively Fifth Street: Murderers, Cheetahs, and Binion's World Series of Poker*, p. 188, while the "asymmetrical warfare" quote is on p. 11. Yardley's observation about suckers is found on p. 52 of *The Education of a Poker Player*. Toki Clark told me her story in an e-mail.

SPADES

Legally Blonde was released in 2001. Some of the dialogue has been paraphrased for the sake of brevity, but the two most important lines ("Don't stamp your little last-season Prada shoes at me, honey"; and "The rules of hair care are simple and finite; any Cosmo girl would have known") are direct quotes from the film.

LESSON 1: *Knowledge Is Power*

Alvarez's "complex pattern of information" is described at p. 50 of *The Biggest Game in Town*.

LESSON 2: *Taking Their Measure*

David Spanier's characterization of *The Hustler* as the best poker movie ever made is found in *Total Poker*, pp. 157–66.

LESSON 3: *Tells*

For a discussion of the research on recognizing falsehoods, see Erica Goode, "To Tell the Truth, It's Awfully Hard to Spot a Liar," *New York Times*, May 11, 1999, p. D1; and Malcolm Gladwell, "The Naked Face," *New Yorker*, August 5, 2002, p. 38.

Sklansky's quote about tells is from *The Theory of Poker*, p. 221; Caro's observations are from *Caro's Book of Tells: The Body Language of Poker*, pp. 12–17 (italics in original); Bellin's quote is from *Poker Nation*, p. 104; Holden's quote is from *Big Deal*, p. 71.

LESSON 4: *Get What You Need*

Johnnie Cochran's description of Mark Fuhrman is on p. 290 of his memoir, *Journey to Justice*; the rest of the quotes are on pp. 290–94.

LESSON 5: *True Lies*

Bellin's psychological explanation for involuntary tells is found on p. 95 of *Poker Nation*. Caro's list of common tells is from "Tips from Mike Caro University," in Doyle Brunson, *Super System 2: A Course in Power Poker*, pp. 167–76.

LESSON 6: *That's Acting*

Caro expounds further on acted tells in *Caro's Book of Tells*, p. 134; his Great Law of Tells is introduced on p. 19. The significance of sighs is explained in "Tips from Mike Caro University," in Brunson, *Super System 2: A Course in Power Poker*, p. 170.

The description of Steven Seagal's acting skills is taken from Michael Konik, *Telling Lies and Getting Paid*, p. 202.

LESSON 7: *Calling Bias*

Caro's description of opposing players—"they're a little bit like snakes"—is found in "Tips from Mike Caro University," in Brunson, *Super System 2: A Course in Power Poker*, 165.

The excerpt from President Clinton's testimony is from Douglas Linder's "Famous American Trials" Web site, http://www.law.umkc.edu/faculty/projects/ftrials/clinton/clintonhome.html.

LESSON 8: *Paying Attention*

The excerpt from the Sacco and Vanzetti trial is from Douglas Linder's "Famous American Trials" Web site, http://www.law.umkc.edu/faculty/projects/ftrials/SaccoV/SaccoV.htm.

LESSON 9: *Reading Value*

Sklansky's views on betting for value are found in *The Theory of Poker*, p. 239.

LESSON 10: *Total Recall*

Brunson explains his use of the word "feel" in *Super System 2*, p. 542.

The excerpt from the Triangle Shirtwaist fire case is from Douglas Linder's "Famous American Trials" Web site, http://www.law.umkc.edu/faculty/projects/ftrials/triangle/trianglefire.html.

LESSON 11: *The Unexpected*

Yardley chronicles his heroic exploits in China at pp. 81–118 of *The Education of a Poker Player*.

LESSON 12: *Local Rules*

The "old cat" story is adapted from Tuttle, *Maverick's Guide to Poker*, pp. 24–25.

LESSON 13: *Showing Your Hand*

By-the-book deposition practice is taught by David Malone and Peter Hoffman in *The Effective Deposition*; the quote is at p. 198. The statistics on settlement are taken from the

National Center for State Courts, "Examining the Work of State Courts," 1994 (1996): 10, cited in Thomas Koenig, "The Shadow Effect of Punitive Damages on Settlements," *Wisconsin Law Review* (1998): 169, 171.

The BATNA concept was developed by Roger Fisher and William Ury in their classic negotiation primer, *Getting to Yes*, first published in 1983.

The story of Jack Straus was first told by Alvarez in *The Biggest Game in Town*. This version is adapted from his more-recent book *Poker: Bets, Bluffs, and Bad Beats*, p. 83.

HEARTS

For a longer version of Mary Corcoran's ordeal, see Steven Lubet, "Dispiriting the Law," *American Lawyer* 26 (August 2004): 146. Referral fees are governed by Rule 1.5 of the American Bar Association's *Model Rules of Professional Conduct*, which provides certain conditions and requires that they be reasonable.

LESSON I: *Lying*

Holden's quote about character is from *Big Deal*, pp. 91–92.

The details of the Bill Clinton saga are from his autobiography, *My Life*. Parts of this section were previously published in Lubet, "The Clinton Miscalculus: If the President Had Trusted His Lawyer, History Might Be Different," *American Lawyer* 26 (November 2004): 170.

Bellin's quote about poker and relationships is from *Poker Nation*, p. 206; Michael Konik's quote about lying and losing is from *Telling Lies and Getting Paid*, p. 174; Mike Caro's contrasting quote about the utility of lying in poker is from *Super System 2*, p. 157.

The description of Joseph Cowell's riverboat memoir is adapted from Alvarez, *Poker*, pp. 36–37; and Spanier, *Total Poker*, pp. 58–59. Yardley describes how Monty caught a cheater in *The Education of a Poker Player*, pp. 22–23. Alvarez quotes W. C. Fields and Walter Mattheau in *Poker*, p. 28.

LESSON 3: *Scamming*

Alvarez's observation about bluffing and acting is found in *Poker*, p. 82.

Rule 3.4(e), American Bar Association, *Model Rules of Professional Conduct*, prohibits scamming by "stating or alluding" to anything not supported by admissible evidence.

LESSON 4: *Banking the Proceeds*

For the context of Greg Raymer's prescient quote, see http://www.legalunderground.com/2004/05/greg_raymer_was.html. His biography comes from the Web site "Card-Sharx," http://www.card-sharx.com/greg-fossilman-raymer-biography.html. The quotes about his WSOP victory are from Michael Kaplan's profile, "The Poker Ace," in *Cigar Aficionado*, available on-line at http://www.cigaraficionado.com/Cigar/CA_Profiles/People_Profile/0,2540,189,00.html.

Richard Nixon's card-playing exploits are described in Spanier's *Total Poker*, pp. 73–74.

LESSON 5: *The Right Stuff*

Henry Clay's showdown with Daniel Webster is described in Spanier's *Total Poker*, pp. 81–83; Alvarez's commentary is on p. 72 of *Poker*.

LESSON 6: *Moral Hazards*

Alvarez explains the "endless game" concept on p. 75 of *The Biggest Game in Town*.

Aggregate settlements are prohibited by the American Bar Association's *Model Rules of Professional Conduct*, Rule 1.8(g).

LESSON 7: *Self-Control*

Caro's observation—"you don't get paid to win pots"—is in "Tips from Mike Caro University," in Doyle Brunson, *Super System 2: A Course in Power Poker*, p. 128.

Glen Kanwit's story is from an e-mail.

LESSON 8: *Beginner's Luck*

Chris Moneymaker tells his own lucky story in *Moneymaker: How an Amateur Poker Player Turned $40 into $2.5 Million at the World Series of Poker*, pp. 151–52. Commentary is added in a book review by A. J. Jacobs, "Not Bluffing," *New York Times*, May 8, 2005, sec. 7, p. 21.

LESSON 9: *You Gotta Have Heart*

Katy Lederer's family saga is told in her memoir, *Poker Face*, with the story of her sister's second thoughts at pp. 149–50.

LESSON 10: *Cards Speak*

Holden's "cards speak" story is found on pp. 216–17 of *Big Deal*. My rendition of the story adds suits to some of the cards, so that the graphics will make more sense, without changing the nature of the hand.

LESSON 11: *Cross-Examination Does Not Mean Angry Examination*

Brunson's explanation of aggression is found in *Super System*, pp. 442–43 (ellipses and emphases in the original).

Chris Moneymaker's candid appraisal of his losing hand is in his memoir, *Moneymaker*, p. 155.

For more on the Martha Stewart case, see Jeffrey Toobin, "A Bad Thing: Why Did Martha Stewart Lose?" *New Yorker*, March 22, 2004, p. 60. Portions of my description of the trial were previously published in Lubet, "Oyez, O Muse," *American Lawyer* 26 (June 2004): 118.

Bibliography

BOOKS

Alvarez, A. *The Biggest Game in Town*. San Francisco: Chronicle, 2002.

———. *Poker: Bets, Bluffs, and Bad Beats*. San Francisco: Chronicle, 2004.

American Bar Association. *Model Rules of Professional Conduct*. Chicago: American Bar Association, 2004. http://www .abanet.org/cpr/mrpc/mrpc_home.html.

Bellin, Andy. *Poker Nation: A High-Stakes, Low-Life Adventure into the Heart of a Gambling Country*. New York: Harper, 2003.

Brunson, Doyle. *Doyle Brunson's Super System: A Course in Power Poker*. New York: Cardoza, 1979.

———. *Doyle Brunson's Super System 2: A Course in Power Poker*. New York: Cardoza, 2005.

Caro, Mike. *Mike Caro's Book of Tells: The Body Language of Poker*. Secaucus, NJ: Stuart, 1984.

Clinton, Bill. *My Life*. New York: Knopf, 2004.

Cochran, Johnnie L. *Journey to Justice*. New York: One World/ Ballantine, 1996.

270   Darden, Christopher, and Jess Walter. *In Contempt*. New York:
■   HarperCollins, 1996.

Federal Rules of Civil Procedure (2006).

Fisher, Roger, and William Ury. *Getting to Yes: Negotiating Agreement without Giving In*. New York: Penguin, 1983.

Fletcher, George P. *A Crime of Self-Defense: Bernhard Goetz and the Law on Trial*. Chicago: University of Chicago Press, 1990.

Holden, Anthony. *Big Deal: One Year as a Professional Poker Player*. London: Abacus, 2002.

Holland, Merlin, ed. *The Real Trial of Oscar Wilde*. New York: Fourth Estate, 2003.

Konik, Michael. *Telling Lies and Getting Paid: Gambling Stories*. Guilford, CT: Lyons, 2002.

Lederer, Katy. *Poker Face: A Girlhood among Gamblers*. New York: Three Rivers, 2004.

Lubet, Steven. *Modern Trial Advocacy: Analysis and Practice*, 3d ed. South Bend, IN: National Institute for Trial Advocacy, 2004.

McManus, James. *Positively Fifth Street: Murderers, Cheetahs, and Binion's World Series of Poker*. New York: Picador, 2004.

Malone, David M., and Peter T. Hoffman. *The Effective Deposition: Techniques and Strategies That Work*. South Bend, IN: National Institute for Trial Advocacy, 2001.

Moneymaker, Chris. *Moneymaker: How an Amateur Poker Player Turned $40 into $2.5 Million at the World Series of Poker*. New York: Harper Entertainment, 2005.

Phillips, Larry. *Zen and the Art of Poker: Timeless Secrets to Transform Your Game*. New York: Plume, 1999.

Sklansky, David. *The Theory of Poker*. Henderson, NV: Two plus Two, 1994.

Spanier, David. *Total Poker*. London: High Stakes, 1977.

Tolstoy, Leo. *Anna Karenina* [1878]. New York: Penguin (Richard Pevear and Larissa Volokhonsky, trans.), 2001.

Tuttle, Charles E. *Maverick's Guide to Poker*. Boston: Tuttle, 1994.

von Neumann, John, and Oskar Morgenstern. *Theory of Games and Economic Behavior*. Hoboken, NJ: Wiley, 1953.

Warren, Ken. *Winner's Guide to Texas Hold'em Poker*. New York: Cardoza, 1995.

Webster's New Universal Unabridged Dictionary, 2d ed. Barnes & Noble, 1983.

Yardley, Herbert O. *The American Black Chamber* [1931]. Mattituck, NY: Amereon, 1981.

——. *The Education of a Poker Player*. New York: Simon & Schuster, 1957.

ARTICLES

Gladwell, Malcolm. "The Naked Face." *New Yorker*, August 5, 2002, at 38.

Goode, Erica. "To Tell the Truth, It's Awfully Hard to Spot a Liar." *New York Times*, May 11, 1999, at D1.

Jacobs, A. J. "Not Bluffing." *New York Times*, May 8, 2005, at sec. 7, 21.

Lubet, Steven. "The Clinton Miscalculus: If the President Had Trusted His Lawyer, History Might Be Different." *American Lawyer* 26 (November 2004): 170.

——. "Dispiriting the Law." *American Lawyer* 26 (August 2004): 146.

——. "Lawyers' Poker." *University of Miami Law Review* 57 (2003): 283.

——. "Oyez, O Muse." *American Lawyer* 26 (June 2004): 118.

National Center for State Courts. "Examining the Work of State Courts, 1994" (1996): 10. Cited in Thomas Koenig, "The Shadow Effect of Punitive Damages on Settlements." *Wisconsin Law Review* (1998): 169, 171.

Shulman, Allyn Jaffrey. "Doyle Brunson: Five Decades of Poker and Still Going Strong." *Card Player Magazine*, August 27, 2004.

Toobin, Jeffrey. "A Bad Thing: Why Did Martha Stewart Lose?" *New Yorker*, March 22, 2004, at 60.

———. "The Unasked Question: Why the Diallo Case Missed the Point." *New Yorker*, March 6, 2000, at 38.

FILMS

A Big Hand for the Little Lady. Directed by Fielder Cook. Eden Productions, 1966.

The Hustler. Directed by Robert Rossen. Twentieth-Century Fox, 1961.

Legally Blonde. Directed by Robert Luketic. MGM/UA, 2001.

The Music Man. Directed by Morton DaCosta. Warner Brothers, 1962.

My Cousin Vinnie. Directed by Jonathan Lynn. Twentieth-Century Fox, 1992.

My Little Chickadee. Directed by Edward F. Cline. Universal Pictures, 1940.

Rounders. Directed by John Dahl. Miramax, 1998.

The Ten Commandments of Cross-Examination (Basic Concepts in the Law of Evidence series). Produced by the National Institute for Trial Advocacy, 1975.

INDEX

Adams, John Quincy, 214
Addington, Crandall, 122–23
Alto, Jesse, 94–96
Alvarez, A., 43–44, 69, 94–96,
    213
  on betting, 135
  on bluffing, 206
  on folding, 115–16
  on game length, 215–16
  on luck, 49
Anna Karenina, 241–42

Bailey, F. Lee, 74–77, 149–51
Baldwin, Bobby, 50, 122–23
Beck, Phillip, 87–89
Bellin, Andy, 20–22, 196
  on betting, 80–83
  on bluffing, 91–93
  on chasing cards, 41
  on stakes, 68–70
  on steaming, 49–50
  on tells, 145–46, 151–52
Bennett, Robert, 192–96

A Big Hand for the Little Lady,
    203–6
Binion, Benny, 37, 40
Bloch, Emmanuel, 54–56
Brunson, Doyle "Texas Dolly,"
    33, 56, 57–59, 94, 169–70
  on aggression, 61–63, 236,
    241
  on bluffing, 104–5
  folding, 115–16
Bryan, William Jennings, 45–48
Bush, George W., 87–89

Caro, Mike, 111–15, 191
  on calling, 158
  on folding, 218–19
  on lying, 196
  on tells, 142, 145, 152–57, 162
Carson, Edward, 100–103,
    167–68
Chan, Johnny, 123–24, 170
Clark, Toki, 128–29
Clarke, Sir Edward, 167–68

Clay, Henry, 213–15
Clinton, William Jefferson,
    159–61, 192–96
Cochran, Johnnie, 74–77,
    149–51
Corboy & Demetrio, 188–90
Corcoran, Mary, 188–90
Cowell, Joseph, 197–99
Crowe, Robert, 12–15

Damon, Matt, 146
Dandalos, Nick, 36–40
Darden, Christopher, 74–77
Darrow, Clarence, 12–15, 45–48,
    57–58
Diallo, Amadou, 117–18
Dowd, Joseph, 188–90, 232

Eisenhower, Dwight, 212

Fields, W. C., 20, 199
Fonda, Henry, 204
Frankfurter, Felix, 165
Fuhrman, Mark, 149–51

Gambini, Vinnie, 220–26
Gladwell, Malcolm, 143
Goetz, Bernhard, 124–26
Gore, Al, 87–89

Hill, Harold, 239–40
Hiss, Alger, 24–28
Holden, Anthony, 64, 144, 191,
    232–33
The Hustler, 138–41, 146

Jacobs, A. J., 228

Jones, Paula, 192

Kanwit, Glen, 219–24
Konik, Michael, 196

Lederer, Howard, 230–32,
    242–43
Lederer, Katy, 230–32
Legally Blonde, 132–34
Leopold, Nathan, 12–15
Lewinsky, Monica, 192–96
Lincoln, Abraham, 51–53,
    140–41
Loeb, Richard, 12–15
Lombardi, Vince, 12

Matthau, Walter, 199
McAnarney, Jeremiah, 163–69
McDermott, Mike, 146–51,
    170–71
McManus, James, 8, 40, 127–29,
    233–34
Moneymaker, Chris, 226–29,
    242–43
Morgenstern, Oskar, 91
Morrison, Alan, 105–107
Moss, Johnny, 37–41
The Music Man, 239–40
My Cousin Vinnie, 220–26

Nixon, Richard, 210–12, 215

Pearson, Puggy, 49–50, 94,
    120–21
Pesci, Joe, 220
Preston, Thomas "Amarillo
    Slim," 41, 115–16, 120–21

Raymer, Greg "Fossilman,"
 209-10
Rosenberg, Ethel, 53-56
Rosenberg, Julius, 53-56
Rounders, 146-51, 170-71

Sacco, Nicola, 163-69
Scopes, John, 45-48
Seidel, Eric, 123-24, 170
Simpson, O. J., 74-77, 149-51
Sklansky, David, 64, 78-79
 on betting, 81, 166
 on controlling bluffs, 109
 on reading your opponent,
  142
 on semi-bluffing, 97-98
 on slow playing, 85-86
Spanier, David, 138-39, 146,
 211-12, 213
Starr, Ken, 195-96
Steuer, Max, 173-75
Stewart, Martha, 243-46
Straus, Jack "Treetop," 94-97,
 184-86

Tolstoy, Leo, 241-42
Tomei, Marisa, 221

Toobin, Jeffrey, 246
Triangle Shirtwaist Company,
 171-75
Truman, Harry, 212

Vanzetti, Bartolomeo, 163-69
von Neumann, John, 91

Warren, Ken, 30
Washington, George, 212
Webster, Daniel, 213-15
Wilde, Oscar, 100-103,
 166-68
Williams, Merrill, 105-7
Witherspoon, Reese, 132-34
Woods, Elle, 132-34
Woodward, Joanne, 204

Yardley, Herbert O., 41-43, 48,
 64
 on bluffing, 105
 on calling, 157-58
 on cheating, 200-202
 on folding, 57, 60, 127-28
 on slow playing, 86-97
 on stakes, 67-68
 on staying alert, 175-78